Compiled from the archives of *Sheet Music Magazine*
with special thanks to Kirk Miller

Project Manager: Sy Feldman
Production Coordinator: Donna Salzburg
Original sheet music covers courtesy of Sandy Marrone, used by permission
Cover Design: Martha Lucia Ramirez

Contents

AFTER YOU'VE GONE

Judy Garland

Although Al Jolson introduced this favorite standard at the Winter Garden Theater and later recorded it for the 1949 film, Jolson Sings Again, *the first chart appearance of the tune was with a 1918 recording by Henry Burr and Albert Campbell. Burr and Campbell's version was very successful, reaching the penultimate position; the following year, however, a recording by Marion Harris did even better, capturing the top spot. During the same period, Sophie Tucker was encouraging the song's success with her vaudevillian performances and, later, with her 1929 top-ten record. Other versions over the years, including Benny Goodman's (1935 and in the 1946 film,* Make Mine Music*), Judy Garland's (*For Me And My Gal, *1942), Louis Armstrong's (1932 and in 1959's* The Five Pennies*), and Leland Palmer's (in Bob Fosse's* All That Jazz, *1979) have ensured that the song will remain popular long after we've all gone away.*

Words by
HENRY CREAMER

Music by
TURNER LAYTON

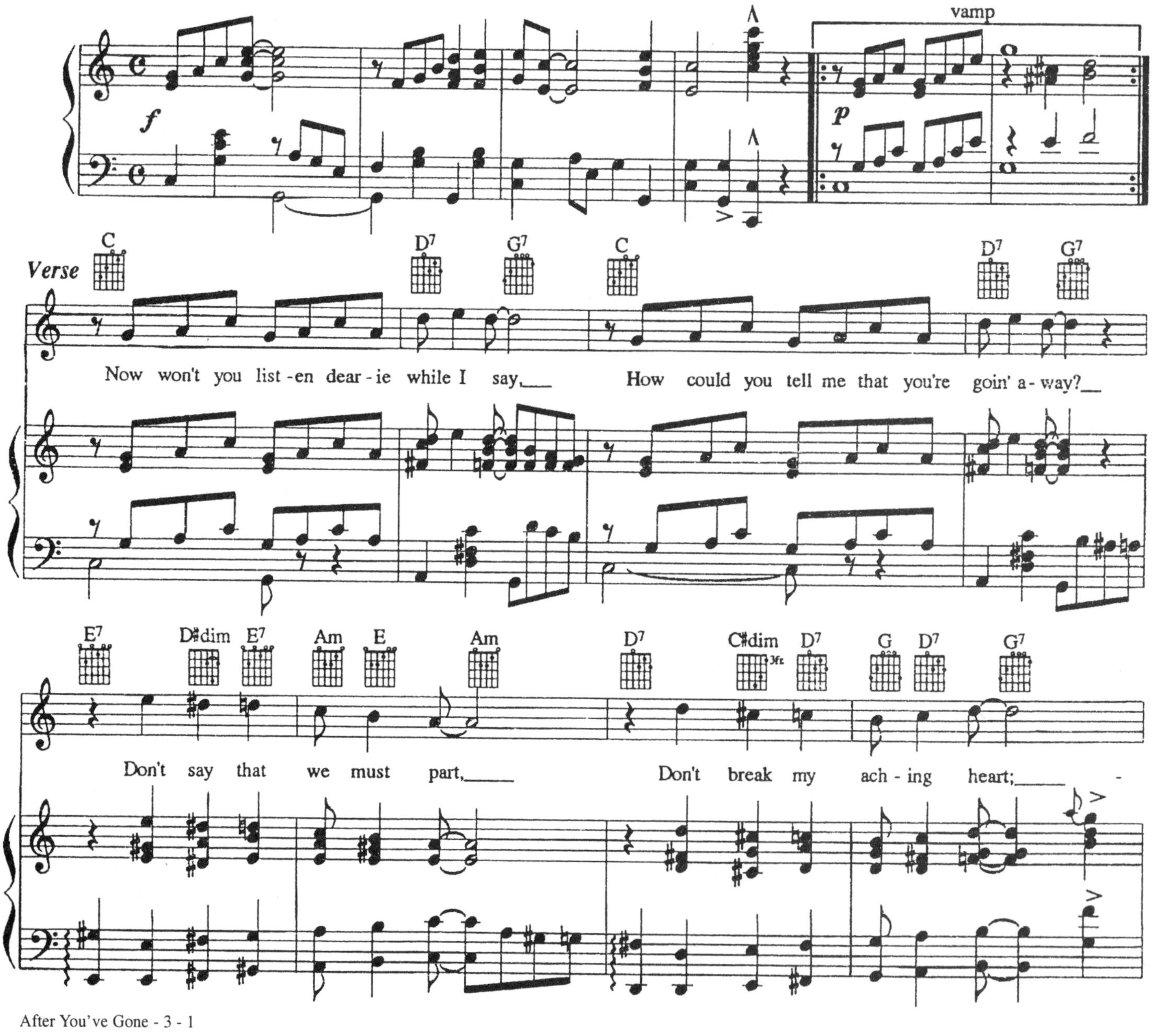

f

vamp

p

Verse

C D7 G7 C D7 G7

Now won't you list - en dear - ie while I say, How could you tell me that you're goin' a - way?

E7 D♯dim E7 Am E Am D7 C♯dim D7 G D7 G7

Don't say that we must part, Don't break my ach - ing heart;

C
D7
G7
C7
F
You know I've loved you tru - ly man - y years,
Loved you night and day;
F♯dim
C
D9
4fr.
G7
C
C+
How can you leave me, can't you see my tears?
List - en while I say:
Chorus:
F
Dm7(♭5)
3fr.
C
A7
Af - ter you've gone, and left me cry - ing; Af - ter you've gone, There's no de - ny - ing;
Af - ter I'm gone, af - ter we break up; Af - ter I'm gone, You're gon - na wake up;
p
mf
D9
4fr.
G7
C
you'll feel blue, You'll feel sad, You'll miss the dear - est pal you've
you will find, You were blind, To let some - bod - y come and

C7 F Dm7(♭5) C
ev - er had; There'll come a time, now don't for - get it, There'll come a time,
change your mind; Af - ter the years, we've been to - geth - er, Their joy and tears,
A7 Dm A7 Dm Dm7(♭5)
when you'll re - gret it; Some day, when you grow lone - ly,
all kinds of wea - ther; Some day, blue and down - heart - ed,
C E7 Am D7 C
Your heart will break like mine and you'll want me on - ly, Af - ter You've Gone,
You'll long to be with me right back where you start - ed; Af - ter I'm gone,
G7 C G7 1. C Bdim C7 2. C
Af - ter You've Gone a - way.
Af - ter I'm gone a - way.

AIN'T MISBEHAVIN'

Written in 1929, this song was introduced in the Broadway revue Hot Chocolates. *In 1978 it became the centerpiece of the Broadway musical* Ain't Misbehavin'. *It starred the sassy Nell Carter and racked up 1,604 performances.*

Words by
ANDY RAZAF

Music by
THOMAS "FATS" WALLER and HARRY BROOKS

C Am D9 Cm6 E (B bass) F#7 B7 E G7
My love was giv - en, heart and soul,__ So it can stand the test.
And made you mine a - lone for keeps,_ Dit - to to all you say.
rit.
Moderately
Chorus:
C C (E bass) Dm7 G9 C C7 (G bass)
No one to talk with, all by my - self, No one to walk with, but
mf
a tempo
F Fm C (E bass) Am7 Dm7 G9
I'm hap - py on___ the shelf, Ain't Mis - be - hav - in', I'm sav - in' my love for
E7 A7 D9 G7+5 C C (E bass)
you.
I know for cer - tain

Dm7
G9
C
C7
(G bass)
F
Fm
the one I love, I'm thru with flirt - in', it's just you I'm think - in' of,
C
(E bass)
Am7
Dm7
G9
C
C7
F#dim
Fm
Ain't Mis - be - hav - in', I'm sav - in' my love for you.
C
(E bass)
E7
Am
F
(A bass)
Like Jack Hor - ner in the cor - ner,
Am6
A7
G
(D bass)
G6
(D bass)
don't go no - where, What do I care, Your kiss - es

Am7
D9
G7
A7
D9
G7
are worth wait - in' for, be - lieve me.
C
C (E bass)
Dm7
G9
C
C7 (G bass)
I don't stay out late, don't care to go, I'm home a - bout eight, just
F
Fm
C (E bass)
Am7
Dm7
G9
me and my ra - di - o, Ain't Mis - be - hav - in', I'm sav - in' my love for
C
1.
C♯dim
Dm7
G9
2.
F7
C
you.

Alice Faye and Tyrone Power

ALEXANDER'S RAGTIME BAND

This Irving Berlin favorite has been recorded by more artists than can be listed here. Its first recording in 1911 by Arthur Collins and Byron Harlan reached the top of the charts, and the 1938 recording by Bing Crosby and Connie Boswell was another chart-topper. The award winning title film starred Alice Faye, Tyrone Power, Ethel Merman and Don Ameche.

Words and Music by
IRVING BERLIN

Moderato

f

C C7 F Dm7 G7

VOICE

Oh, ma hon-ey, Oh, ma hon-ey, Bet-ter hur-ry and let's me-an-der,
Oh, ma hon-ey, Oh, ma hon-ey, There's a fid-dle with notes that screech-es,

mp

C D7 G7

Ain't you go-in', Ain't you go-in', To the lead-er man, rag-ged me-ter man?
Like a chick-en, Like a chick-en, And the clar-in-et is a col-ored pet,

C
C7
F
Dm7
G7
Oh, ma hon - ey, Oh, ma hon - ey, Let me take you to Al - ex - an - der's
Come and lis - ten, Come and lis - ten, To a class - i - cal band what's peach - es,
C
C7
F
Cdim
C
G7
C
C7
grand stand, brass band, Ain't you com - in' a - long?
come now, some - how, Bet - ter hur - ry a - long.
CHORUS
F
Come on and hear, Come on and hear ALEX -
mp - mf
C7
F
Bb
AN - DER'S RAG-TIME BAND, Come on and hear, Come on and

F
hear, It's the best band in the land, They can play a bu-gle call like you
C
Cdim
nev-er heard be-fore, So nat-ur-al that you want to go to war; That's just the
G7
C
C7
F
best-est band what am, hon-ey lamb, Come on a-long, Come on a-
C7
F
long, Let me take you by the hand, Up to the

Bb
man, Up to the man who's the lead - er of the
Bb
F7
Bb
band, And if you care to hear the Swa - nee Riv - er played in
Fdim
F
Fdim
rag - time, Come on and hear, Come on and hear ALEX -
C7
F
Cdim
C7
F
1.
2.
AN - DER'S RAG - TIME BAND. Come on and BAND.

Jimmy Dorsey and Bob Eberly

ALL OR NOTHING AT ALL

Frank Sinatra's first big hit. It is the definitive version, of course. You might, however, recall a different recording by Jimmy Dorsey and His Orchestra with Bob Eberly that was used in the 1981 Jack Lemmon film, Missing.

Lyric by
JACK LAWRENCE

Music by
ARTHUR ALTMAN

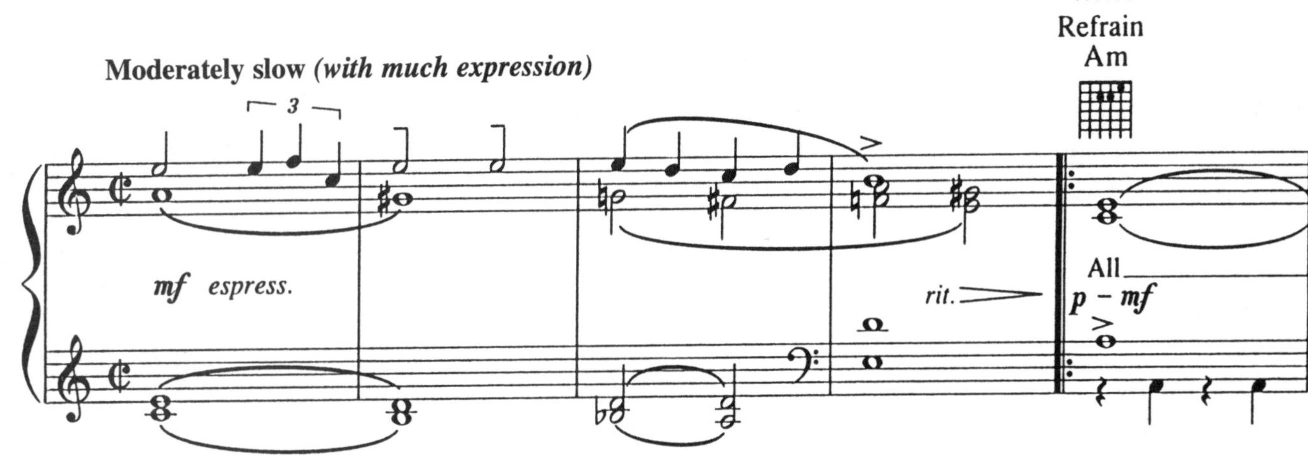

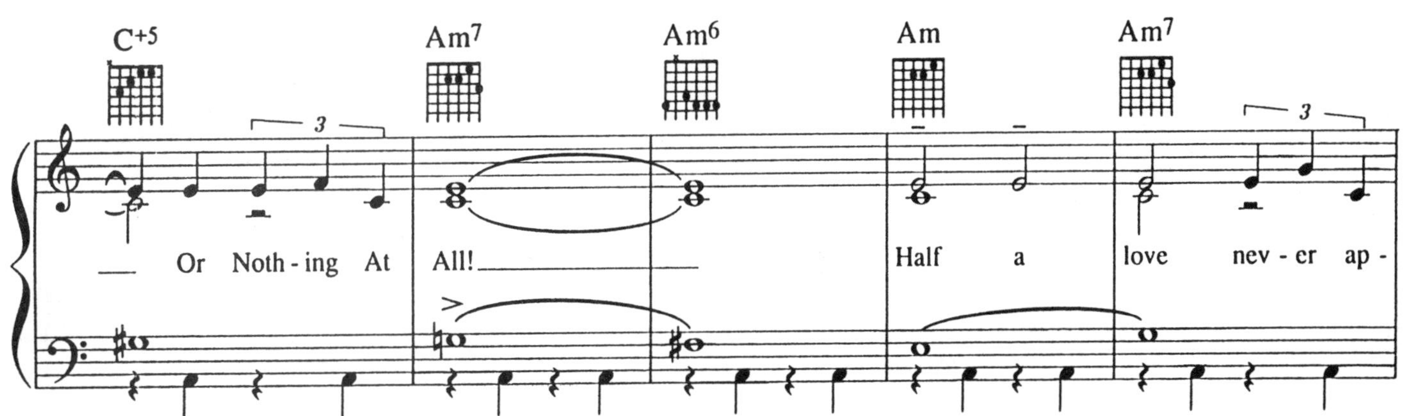

B♭7
B♭6
B♭+5
fr5
B♭7
Gm
Gm6
Dm
3
pealed to me.
If your heart nev - er could yield to me,
G7
G7♭5
G7
Cmaj7
C6
Bm7
E7
then I'd rath - er have noth - ing at all!
Am
C+5
Am7
Am6
Am
3
p
All Or Noth - ing At All!
If it's
Am7
B♭7
B♭6
B♭+5
fr5
B♭7
Gm
Gm6
3
3
love there is no in be - tween.
Why be - gin, then cry for some - thing that

Dm
G7
G7♭5
G7
Cmaj7
C6
might have been. No, I'd rath - er have noth - ing at all.
E♭9
E♭7
A♭
A♭+5
A♭6
A♭+5
A♭
A♭+5
A♭6
E♭7
But, please, don't bring your lips so close to my cheek. Don't
mf espress.
A♭
A♭+5
D♭
A♭
E♭7
Cm6
E♭7
B♭m7
E♭7
smile or I'll be lost be-yond re - call. The kiss in your eyes, the
B♭m7
E♭7
B♭m7
E♭7
B♭m6
C7
Fm
D♭7
touch of your hand makes me weak, and my heart may grow diz - zy and

C7 E7 Am C+5 Am7
fall. And if I fell un - der the spell of your call,
p
Am6 Am Am7 B♭7 B♭6 B♭+5 B♭7
fr5
I would be caught in the un - der - tow.
Gm Gm6 Dm Dm6 E7 Am
fr5
So, you see, I've got to say: No! No! All
molto espress.
Fm6 C E7 C C6
1.
2.
Or Noth - ing At All! All!
f
f

Frank Sinatra

ALL THE WAY

Van Heusen and I never dreamed they would call a film "The Joker Is Wild," so we spent days thinking of the title All The Way! *Of course they didn't use our title, but the song went on to win an Academy Award, thanks to Frank Sinatra!*

Words by
SAMMY CAHN

Music by
JAMES VAN HEUSEN

Slowly

mp

poco rit.

Eb G7+5 Cm

Refrain *(molto espressivo)*

a tempo

mp-mf

When some-bod-y loves you, it's no good un-less {he / she} loves you All The

F9 Bb7 Fm7 Dbm6 Bb7

Way. Hap-py to be near you, when you need some-one to cheer you

Eb
Bbm7
Eb7
Ab
Bb7
Fm6
All The Way. Tall-er than the tall-est tree is,
8va
G7
Cm
Bbm7
Eb7-5
Ab
Bb7
Bdim
That's how it got to feel; Deep-er than the deep blue sea is,
Cm
Cm7
F7
Abm6
Eb
that's how deep it goes, if it's real. When some-bod-y needs you, it's no
rall.
a tempo
G7+5
Cm
F9
good un-less he she needs you All The Way.

Bb7 Fm7 Dbm6 Bb7 Eb Bbm7 Eb7
Through the good or lean years and for all the in be-tween years, Come what may.
8va
Ab Bb7 Fm6 G7 Cm Abm6
Who knows — where the road will lead us? On-ly a fool would say, But
poco rall.
Eb C7 Db9 C7 Cm6 Bb9 Bbm6 C7
if you let me love you, it's for sure I'm gon-na love you All The Way,
a tempo
Abm6 Bb7-5 1. Eb6 Bb7 2. Eb Db9 Eb6
All The Way. Way.
rall.
a tempo
poco rit.
8

Ethel Waters

AM I BLUE?

This all-time standard was introduced by Ethel Waters in the 1929 film On With The Show, *the first all color, all singing film produced by Warner Brothers Studios. It was performed by Barbra Streisand in the 1975 film* Funny Lady, *and in 1985 it was a part of the French production of* Black And Blue, *sung by Sandra-Reaves Phillips while perched on a swing 16 feet above the ground. The American version of* Black And Blue, *was nominated for a Tony Award as best Broadway musical.*

Words by
GRANT CLARKE

Music by
HARRY AKST

Moderately

F C9

Am I blue? Am I blue? Ain't these tears

4fr.

F A7-5 D7 G7 D♭7 C7 F F6 F♯o7 C7 F

in these eyes tel-lin' you? Am I blue?

4fr.

C9 F A7-5 D7 G7 D♭7 C7

You'd be too If each plan with your man done fell through.

F Bb Bbm F Am E7 Dm6
Was a time I was his on-ly one,
E7 Am F#o7 3fr. Gm7 C7
But now I'm the sad and lone-ly one, "Law-dy," Was I gay?
F C9 F F#o7 D7
'til to-day, Now he's gone and we're through,
G7 4fr. Db7 C7 1. F F7 3fr. Gm7 C7 2. F Bb Bbm F
Am I blue? Am I blue? blue?
f
sffz

Ethel Merman

ANYTHING GOES

A favorite of dinner theatres across the nation, and a recent revival at Lincoln Center, Anything Goes *is widely regarded as one of Cole Porter's best scores. Ethel Merman, as one-time evangelist Reno Sweeney, brought down the house in 1934 with this "list" of modern-day lapses in morality.*

Words and Music by
COLE PORTER

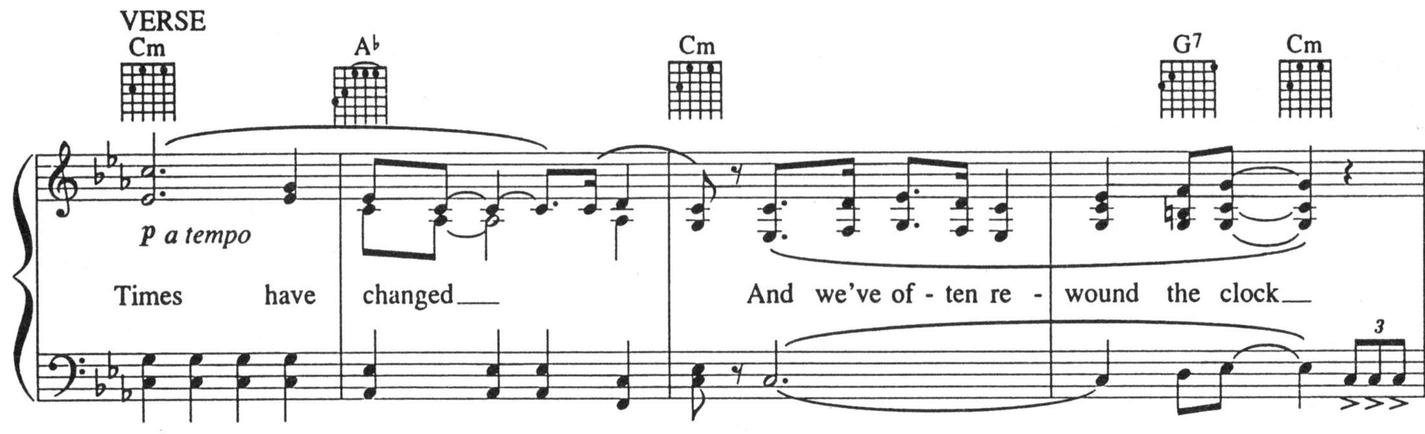

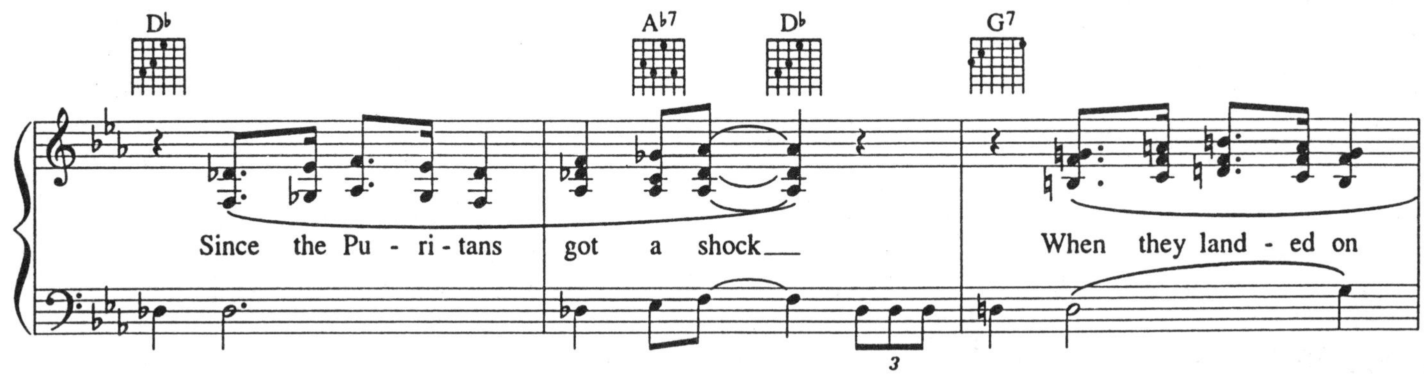

Dm7
G7
C7
Ply - mouth Rock;
If to - day
mf
Fm
C7
Fm
G7
An - y shock they should try to stem,
'Stead of land - ing on
Cm
G7
Cm
G
D7
G7
G6
Ply - mouth Rock Ply - mouth Rock would land on them.
REFRAIN
G7
C
Am
In old - en days a glimpse of stock - ing Was looked on as some - thing shock-
p mf
C7
Dm7
C
Dm7
Fm6
- ing, Now heav - en knows,
An - y - thing

C F6 C G+ C
goes. Good auth - ors too who
mf
Am C7
once knew bet - ter words Now on - ly use four - let - ter words, writ - ing
Dm7 C Dm7 Fm6 C Dm
prose, An - y - thing goes.
C B7 E B9 B7
The world has gone mad to - day And good's bad to - day, And black's
mf
E7 B7 Em
white to - day, And day's night to - day, When most guys to - day That wo - men

REFRAIN 2

When missus Ned McLean (God bless her)
Can get Russian reds to "yes" her,
Then I suppose
Anything goes.
When Rockefeller still can hoard enough money
  to let Max Gordon
Produce his shows,
Anything goes.
The world has gone mad today
And good's bad today,
And black's white today,
And day's night today,
And that gent today,
You gave a cent, today
Once had several chateaux.
When folks who still can ride in jitneys
Find out Vanderbilts and Whitneys
Lack baby-clo'es,
Anything goes.

REFRAIN 3

If Sam Goldwyn can with great conviction
Instruct Anna Sten in diction,
Then Anna shows
Anything goes.
When you hear that Lady Mendl standing up
Now turns a handspring landing upon her toes,
Anything goes.
Just think of those shocks you've got
And those knocks you've got,
And those blues you've got,
From that news you've got,
And those pains you've got,
(If any brains you've got)
From those little radios.
So Missus R., with all her trimmins
Can broadcast a bed from Simmons
'Cause Franklin knows
Anything goes.

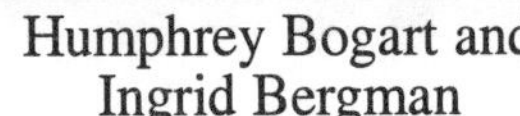

Humphrey Bogart and Ingrid Bergman

AS TIME GOES BY

Premiered by Frances Williams in the 1931 musical Everybody's Welcome, *"As Time Goes By" has since been recorded by over forty different performers—everyone from Rudy Vallee, whose reissue hit no. 1 in 1943, to the Baja Marimba Band. Of course, who isn't familiar with Dooley Wilson's showstopper in the 1942 film classic* Casablanca, *starring Humphrey Bogart and Ingrid Bergman. Mr. Wilson's performance is so highly regarded, it's been featured in many films, like Woody Allen's 1972 comedy* Play It Again, Sam, *and it became a big radio hit in England in 1977.*

Words and Music by
HERMAN HUPFELD

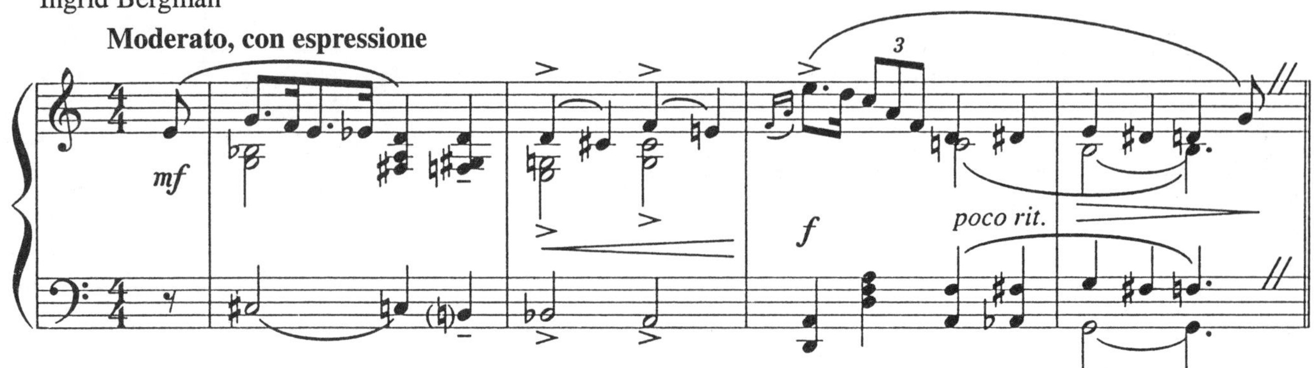

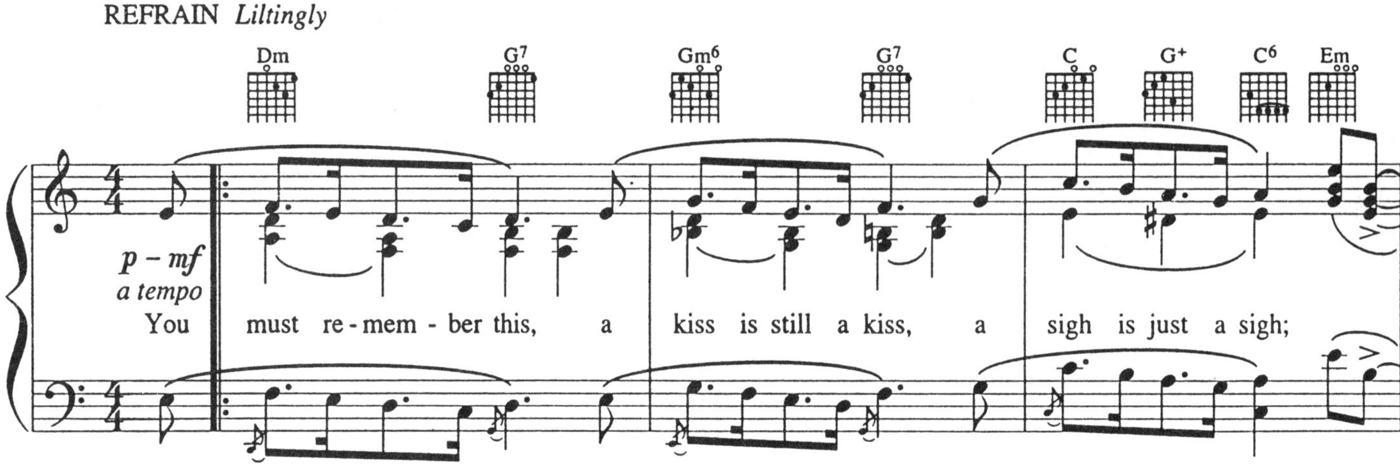

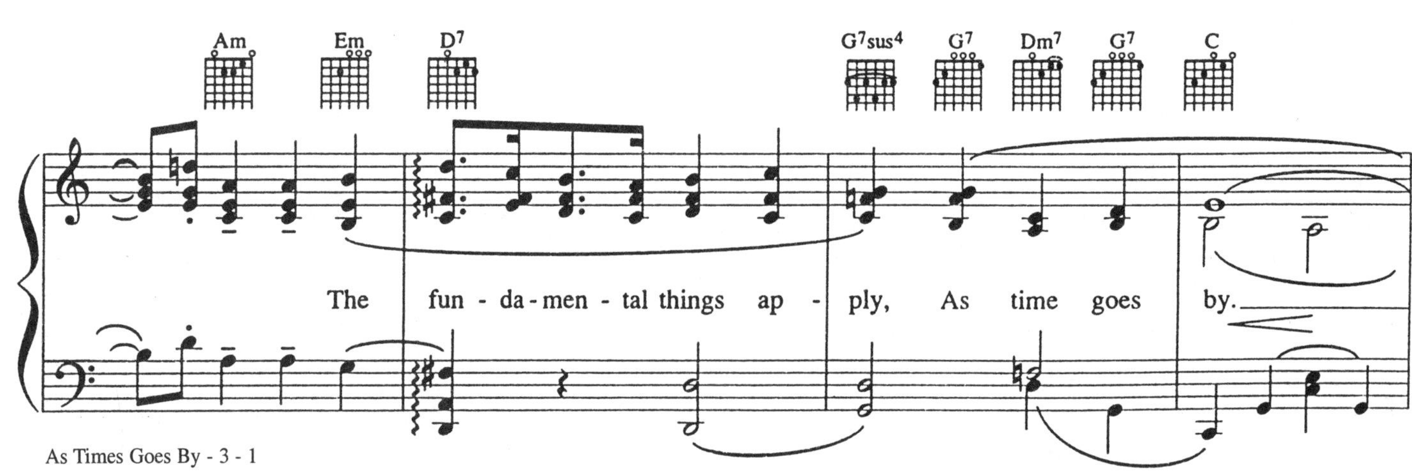

Dm7
G7
Gm6
G7
And when two lov - ers woo, they still say, "I love you," On
C
G+
C6
Em
Am
Em
D7
that you can re - ly; No mat - ter what the fu - ture
G7sus4
G7
Dm7
G7
C
F
Fm
C
C7
F
brings, As time goes by.
Moon - light and love songs
mf – f poco a poco cresc.
A7
Dm
F♯dim
nev - er out of date, Hearts full of pas - sion, jeal - ous - y and hate;

Am
F7
D7
G7
C♯dim
Wo - man needs man and man must have his mate, That no one can de -
poco rit.
G7
Dm7
G7
Gm6
G7
ny. It's still the same old sto - ry, a fight for love and glo - ry, A
p – mf
a tempo
C
G+
C6
Em
Am
Em
D7
case of do or die! The world will al - ways wel - come
C
C♯dim
Dm7
G7
G7+5
1.
C
Am
D7
G7
2.
C
B♭7
C
lov - ers, As time goes by. You by.
f
mf
f
3

J. Carroll Naish, Mario Lanza and Kathryn Grayson

BE MY LOVE

Another Oscar nominee, this time for the 1950 film The Toast Of New Orleans *starring Mario Lanza, Kathryn Grayson and David Niven. Lanza and Grayson's duet was the highlight of the film. This song, which reached the no. 1 spot in 1950 and remained on the charts for an incredible thirty-four weeks, demonstrates Sammy's amazing versatility as a complete lyricist. "The meaning of 'chutzpah' is me at the movie studio singing to Mario Lanza," says Sammy. "And he singing it right back to me was the thrill of a lifetime."*

Words and Music by
SAMMY CAHN and NICHOLAS BRODSZKY

Very moderato tempo

mf

Chorus, very moderate tempo

G

p – mf

BE MY LOVE, for no one else can end this
1.) POUR T'AI - MER, J'ai tout a - ban - don - né sur
2.) (POUR T'AI) - MER, Je veux bâ - tir un monde en

B+ B7 Em C♯° C7♭5

yearn - ing; This need that you and you a - lone cre -
ter - re, Et mon seul bon - heur main - te - nant c'est
rê - ve, Un monde im - mense où nous se - rions tous

B7 E7♭9 Am A♯° G/B
ate. Just fill my arms the way you've filled my dreams,
toi, Seul(e), tu pour - rais, Ché - ri(e), si tu vou - lais,
deux, Je n'ai be - soin Pour fi - xer mon des - tin,
R.H.
D7/A G6 B7/F♯ Em A7 Am7 D11
The dreams that you in - spire with ev - 'ry sweet de - sire.
Cal - mer tous les tour - ments De mon de - sir brû - lant.
Que d'un bon - heur cer - tain Un seul bai - ser, le tien.
D7 E♭7 D7 G F♯°
BE MY LOVE, and with your kiss - es set me
POUR T'AI - MER, Je bra - ve - rais la terre en -
POUR T'AI - MER, Je veux de no - tre vie trop
B+ B7 Em C♯° C7♭5
burn - ing; One kiss is all I need to seal my
tiè - re! Et nul ne pour - ra m'é - loi - gner de
brè - ve Faire une é - ter - ni - té de jours tous

B7 E7♭9 Am A♯o G/B
fate, And hand in hand, we'll find love's prom - ised land. There'll
toi! Sois mon a - mour! Et jus - qu'au der - nier jour Il
bleus. Main dans la main, Vers de beaux len - de-mains, Nous
R.H.
B/A G Bm7/F♯ Em A11 Am9 D7 B°
be no one but you, for me e - ter - nal -
n'y au - ra que toi pour moi Et moi pour
pren - drons les che - mins ri - ants, Où vont gaie -
E7sus E7 A11 Am9 Am11 D13♭9
ly, If you will BE MY
toi Si tu veux être à
ment, Les fous et les a -
1. G6 D7 E♭7 D7 2. G6
LOVE. BE MY LOVE.
moi! 2.) POUR T'AI-
mants.

THE BEST IS YET TO COME

One of the truly classic songs from the Coleman/Leigh collaboration. Both Ella Fitzgerald and Tony Bennett had successful recordings of this gem.

Music by CY COLEMAN

Words by CAROLYN LEIGH

A7
You think you've seen the sun _ but you ain't seen it shine, _
Dm7
G7
Dm7
G7
C
Dm7
D♯dim
C
Wait till the warm-up's un - der way, _ Wait till our lips have met, _
Dm7
G7
Dm7
G7
C
E♭7
D♭6
E♭7
Wait till you see that sun - shine day, _ You ain't seen noth - in' yet! _
A♭
4 fr.
F7
The Best Is Yet To Come _ and babe, won't it be fine, _
B♭7
E♭7
1. A♭
4 fr.
Optional Repeat
The Best Is Yet To Come, _ come the day _ you're mine. _

2. Ab
C7
Interlude
Fm
Db7
mine.
Come_ the day_ you're mine,
mp
Fm6
Db7
Fm
Db7
Fdim
Eb7
I'm gon-na teach you to fly,
We've on-ly tast-ed the
Ab
E7
Db7
E7
Ab
E7
Gm7-5
C7
wine,
We're gon-na drain the cup dry.
Fm
Db7
Fm6
Db7
Wait till your charms are ripe_ for these arms to sur-round,
Fm
Db7
Bb7sus4
Bb7
You think you've flown be-fore,_ but you ain't left the ground.

Ebm7 Fm7 Gb6 Ab7 Db6 Ebm7 Edim Db6
Wait till you're locked in my em - brace, Wait till I draw you near;
Ebm7 Fm7 Gb6 Ab7 Db6 E7 D6 E7
Wait till you see that sun-shine place, Ain't noth - in' like it here!
A
The Best Is Yet To Come and babe, won't it be
mf
F#7 B7
fine; The Best Is Yet To Come,
E7 A
come the day you're mine.

BIDIN' MY TIME

Believe it or not, this sweet song was first introduced by a hillbilly quartet in the 1930 stage musical Girl Crazy. *Ethel Merman made her debut in this show, which ran for 272 performances. When the dust had settled, she had become the reigning queen of American musical comedy.*

Music and Lyrics by
GEORGE GERSHWIN and IRA GERSHWIN

Lazily

Gm 3fr. Gm6 D7sus4 D7 G9

mp

Bb Eb Ab 4fr. Fm7 Bb7

I'm bid - in' my time; 'cause

Eb Ab 4fr. Fm7 Bb7

that's the kind - a guy I'm, { while / be -

Eb C7 Fm7 Abm6 Eb Bb7
oth - er folks grow diz - zy I keep bus - y bid - in' my
gin - nin' on a Mon-day right through Sun-day, bid - in' my
Eb G7 C G7 C
time. Next year, next year
time. Give me, give me,
G7 F C Bb7 Eb
some - thing's bound to hap - pen. This year,
glass tha's full of tink - le. Let me,
Bb7 Eb Cm7 3fr. Cm7-5 F6 F9
this year, I'll just keep on
let me, dream like Rip Van

Bb11 Bb7 Eb Ab 4fr. Fm7 Bb7
nap - pin'. And bid - in' my time. 'cause
Wink - le. He bid-ed his time. and
Eb Ab 4fr. Fm7 Bb7
that's the kind - a guy I'm there's
like that Wink -le guy I'm
Eb C7 Fm7 AbmG
no re - gret-tin' when I'm set - tin'
chas - in' way flies, how the day flies,
Eb Bb7 1. Eb 2. Eb
bid - in' my time. time.
bid - in' my

Tullio Carminati, Franchot Tone and Constance Bennett

THE BOULEVARD OF BROKEN DREAMS

Introduced in the 1934 film musical Moulin Rouge, *starring Constance Bennett and Helen Westley, "The Boulevard Of Broken Dreams" also enjoyed recorded success through disks by Jan Garber and his Orchestra (1934) and Tony Bennett (1950). The 1953 film* Moulin Rouge, *a story about famed artist Toulouse-Lautrec starring Jose Ferrer, included this classic in its score as well.*

Words by
AL DUBIN
Music by
HARRY WARREN

Moderato *(molto expressivo)*

mf *rit.*

D Em7 A7 D Em7 A7 Bm E7 Em7 A7

Night - ly lights are shin - ing bright - ly Feet are trip - ping light - ly while the mus - ic plays.

p a tempo

F#m Bm C#7 F#m Bm C#7 F#m Bm E7 A A7

Mad - ness in the guise of glad - ness O - ver - com - ing sad - ness in a mil - lion ways______ Oh!

Dm
Gm6
A7
REFRAIN
Gay Pa - ree look what you've done to me.
a tempo
I walk a - long the street of
Dm
Gm6
Dm
Gm6
A7
sor - row The Bou - le - vard of Brok - en Dreams Where Gig - o - lo and Gig - o - lette,
p-mf
Dm
can take a kiss with - out re - gret So they for - get their brok - en dreams
Dm6
Dm
Gm6
Dm
You laugh to - night and cry to - mor - row, When you be - hold your shat - tered

Gm6
A7
schemes And Gig - o - lo and Gig - o - lette wake up to find their eyes are wet
Dm
D7
With tears that tell of brok - en dreams.
Here is where you'll al - ways
Cm6
D7
Cm6
D7
Gm
find me Al - ways walk - ing up and down
C7
B♭m6
C7
B♭m6
C7
But I left my soul be - hind me In an old Ca - the - dral

F
A7
Dm
Gm6
town;
The joy that you find here you
bor - row
Dm
Gm6
A7
You can - not keep it long it
seems.
But Gig - o - lo and Gig - o - lette
3
still sing a song and dance a - long
The Bou - le - vard of Brok - en
1
Dm
Bb7
Dreams.
a tempo
A7
fz
I walk a - long the street of
2
Dm
A7
D
Dreams.
8va
f
p

The Nicholas Brothers

CHATTANOOGA CHOO-CHOO

After many failures, Glenn Miller and his Orchestra eventually hit upon that unique reed sound in the late '30s which consequently made them a national treasure. Their magic catapulted "Chattanooga Choo-Choo" into the no. 1 spot for nine weeks and made it the second biggest hit of 1941. Featured in the films It Happened In Sun Valley, Springtime In The Rockies, Sun Valley Serenade *and* The Glenn Miller Story, *it has also been recorded by such diverse musicians as Floyd Cramer (1962), the quintet Harper's Bizarre (1967) and the disco girl group Tuxedo Junction (1978).*

Lyrics by
MACK GORDON
Music by
HARRY WARREN

Moderately, with rhythm

C

Par - don me boy ___ is that the Chat - ta - noo - ga Choo - Choo, ___
I can af - ford ___ to board a Chat - ta - noo - ga Choo - Choo, ___

mf

Dm7 G7 Dm G7

___ Track twen - ty nine, ___ Boy you can gim - me a
___ I've got my fare ___ and just a tri - fle to

1. C Cm6

shine.

2. C Cm6 C7 Gm7 C7

spare. You leave the

F C7 F C7 F C7

Penn - syl - va - nia sta - tion 'bout a quar - ter to four, Read a ma - ga - zine and then you're
When you hear the whis - tle blow - in' eight to the bar Then you know that Ten - nes - see is

F F7 B♭ Fdim F D7

in Bal - ti - more. Din - ner in the din - er, noth - ing could be fin - er
not ver - y far, Shov - el all the coal in, got - ta keep it roll - in'

1. G7-9 D♭7 C7 2. G7-9

than to have your ham - 'n eggs in Car - o - li - na. Woo, woo, Chat - ta - noo - ga

C7 F G7 C Cm6

there you are.

C

There's gon - na be a cer - tain par - ty at the sta - tion

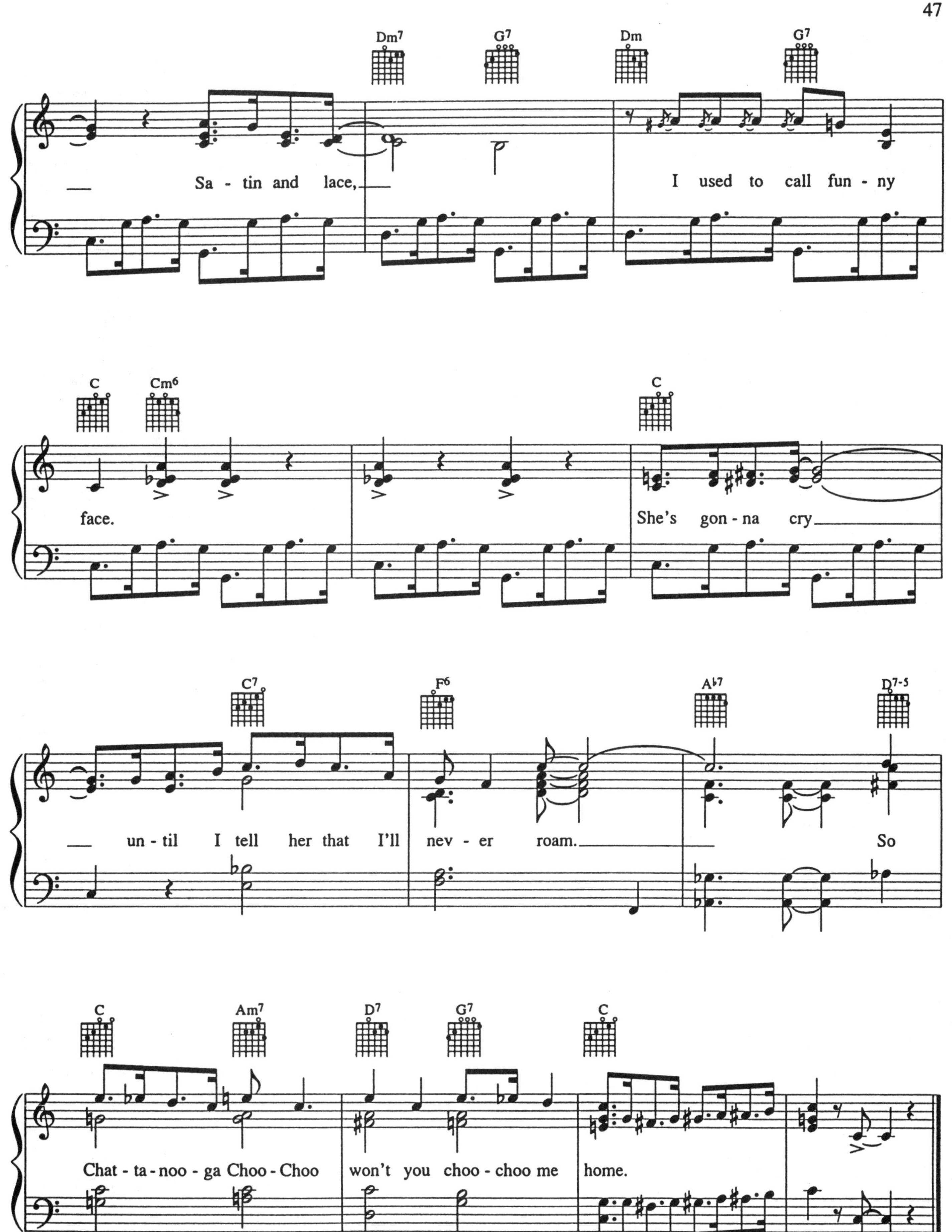
Dm7
G7
Dm
G7
Sa - tin and lace,
I used to call fun - ny
C
Cm6
C
face.
She's gon - na cry
C7
F6
A♭7
D7-5
un - til I tell her that I'll nev - er roam.
So
C
Am7
D7
G7
C
Chat - ta - noo - ga Choo - Choo won't you choo - choo me home.

Frank Sinatra

COME FLY WITH ME

A made-to-order swingin' single for Sinatra, this title became the basis for his 1958 album (Capitol 920). The album held the No. 1 chart position for 5 weeks.

Words by
SAMMY CAHN
Music by
JAMES VAN HEUSEN

Andante

mp

Verse

G7 C G7 C G7 C G Am7

mp

When dad and moth - er dis - cov - ered one an - oth - er, They dreamed of the day when they

G Fmaj7 C Fm6 C Dm C F

rall. *poco accel.*

Would love and hon - or and o - bey. And dur - ing all their mod - est spoon - ing,

G
G9
Em7
Am
Cmaj7
Am6
C
They'd blush and speak of hon - ey - moon - ing.
And if your mem - o - ry re - calls,
D7
Dm7
Fm6
G7
G7♭5
G7+5
C
G7
rall.
They spoke of Ni - ag - 'ra Falls.
But to - day, my dar - ling, to -
tempo primo
C
Am
E+
Am7
D7
G7
Dm7
G7
day, When you meet the one you love, you say;
mf
poco rit.
(rhythmic)
Moderately, with a strong beat
G7
Cmaj9
C6
Cmaj9
C6
Cdim
Dm
Dm7
G7
Refrain
Come Fly With Me! Let's fly! Let's fly a - way! If
mp - mf

Cmaj9 C6 Cmaj9 C6 C7 Fmaj9 C B♭9
you can use some ex - ot - ic booze, there's a bar in far Bom - bay, Come
(views)
Cmaj7 C6 F9 Dm7 G7 E7 A7-9 D9 G7
fr5
Fly With Me! Let's fly! Let's fly a - way! Come
Cmaj9 C6 Cmaj9 C6 Cdim Dm Dm7 G7
Fly With Me! Let's float down to Pe - ru! In
Cmaj7 C6 Cmaj7 C6 C7 Fmaj9 F B♭9
Lla - ma Land there's a one man band and he'll toot his flute for you, Come

Cmaj7
C6
F9
Dm7
G7
C
F7
C
Fly With Me! Let's take off in the blue! (Once I get you)
A♭
A♭+
D♭maj7
D♭6
B♭m
B♭m7
E♭7
mf
Up there! Where the air is rar - i - fied, We'll just glide,
B♭m7
E♭7
A♭
A♭+
A♭6
D♭
star - ry - eyed. (Once I get you) Up there! I'll be hold - ing
G
B♭m6
Bdim
Am7
D7
Am7
D7
G7
B♭m6
F
you so near, You may hear, An - gels cheer, 'cause

G7 B♭7 Dm G7 Cmaj9 C6 Cmaj9 C6 Cdim Dm Dm7
poco rall.
a tempo
we're to - geth - er. Weath - er wise, it's such a love - ly day!
G7 Cmaj7 C6 Cmaj7 C6 C7 Fmaj9 F B♭9
Just say the words and we'll beat the birds down to A - ca - pul - co Bay. It's
Cmaj7 C6 F9 Dm7 G7 Gm6 B♭7 A7 D9 D7
fr5
per - fect for a fly - ing hon - ey - moon, they say; Come Fly With Me! Let's fly.
1.
2.
Dm7 G7 C6 Dm7 F7 G7 C6 C
Let's fly a - way! Come way!
mf

DREAM A LITTLE DREAM OF ME

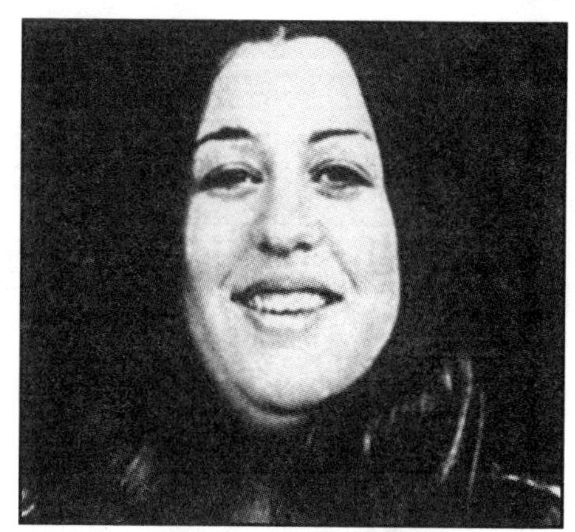

(Mama) Cass Elliot

Freud, Jung and...Gus Kahn! O.K., so it's a bit of a stretch, but the wordsmith of "A Million Dreams," "You Stepped Out Of A Dream," "Last Night I Dreamed You Kissed Me," "My Isle Of Golden Dreams" and many more such dreamy numbers certainly deserves a place in the pantheon of great dream analysts. For interpretations of this illuminating example, refer to recordings by Wayne King, Jack Owens, Frankie Laine, and (Mama) Cass Elliot.

Words and Music by
FABIAN ANDRÉ, GUS KAHN
and WILBUR SCHWANDT

Moderately

mf

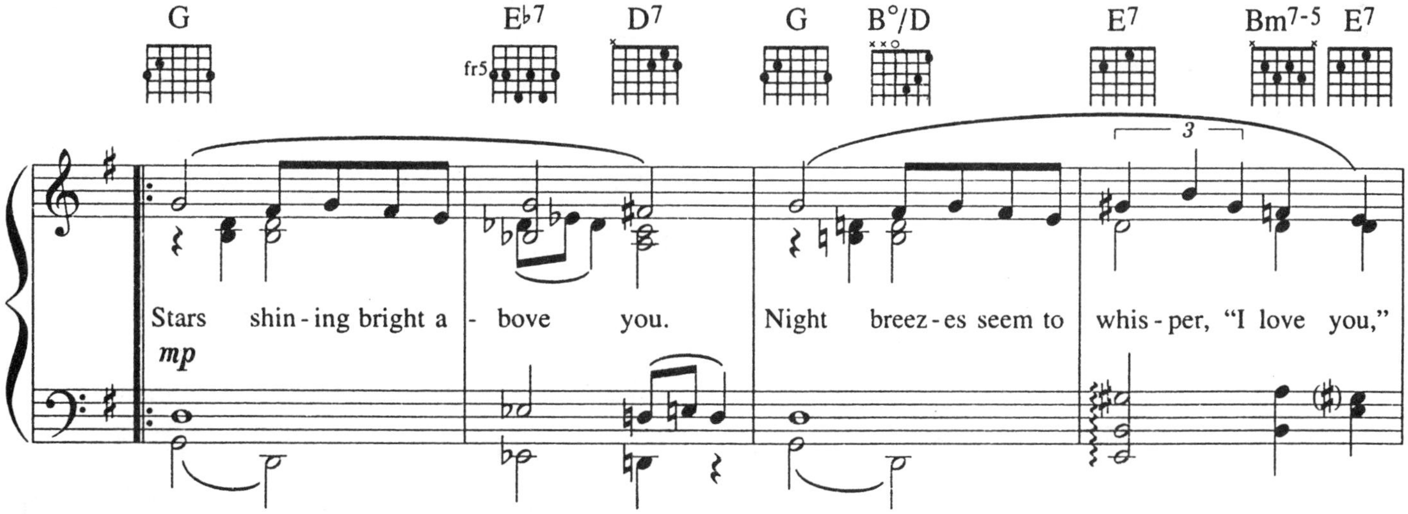

G Eb7 D7 G B°/D E7 Bm7-5 E7

mp

Stars shin - ing bright a - bove you. Night breez - es seem to whis - per, "I love you,"

Am Am7 Am7-5 G A9 D7
Birds sing-ing in the syc-a-more tree, "Dream A Lit-tle Dream Of Me."
G B°/D E♭7 D7 G B°/D E7 Bm7-5 E7
fr5
Say "night-ie-night" and kiss me, Just hold me tight and tell me you'll miss me;
3
Am Am7 Am7-5 G Cm7 D7 G C6 G B♭7/F
While I'm a-lone and blue as can be, Dream A Lit-tle Dream Of Me;
E♭ E♭6 B♭7 E♭ E♭6 B♭7 B♭dim B♭7
fr5 fr5 fr5 fr5
Stars fad-ing, but I lin-ger on, dear, Still crav-ing your kiss;
3

E♭ E♭6 B♭7 E♭
fr5
I'm longing to linger till dawn, dear, Just saying
D7 Em/D Cmaj7/D D7 G B°/D E♭7 D7
this; Sweet dreams till sunbeams find you,
G B°/D E7 Bm7-5 E7 Am Am7
Sweet dreams that leave all worries behind you, But in your dreams what
Am7-5 G Cm7 D7 G E♭7 D7 G
1. 2.
ever they be, Dream A Little Dream Of Me. Me.
p
3

Leslie Caron and Gene Kelly in
An American In Paris

EMBRACEABLE YOU

The question is: Who hasn't performed this gorgeous classic? It was introduced in the 1929 Gershwin musical East Is West, *but gained great success in* Girl Crazy *(1930), and, in* Crazy For You *(1992). Aside from a slew of recordings, including recent Bobby Short and Michael Feinstein releases, "Embraceable You" has also been a prominent addition to many film scores, such as 1951's Oscar-winning* An American In Paris *(by Gene Kelly).*

Music and Lyrics by
GEORGE GERSHWIN and
IRA GERSHWIN

Whimsically

G

p leisurely

Doz - ens of girls would storm — up; I had to lock my door.

D7

mf

p smoothly

F#m D7 Eb9 D7 G Am7 D7

Some - how I could - n't warm — up To one be - fore.

G
F#7
What was it that con - trolled ___ me?
What kept my love - life
B
F#7
B
lean?
My in - tu - i - tion told ___ me You'd come
Am7
G
Em
A9
Em
A9
on the scene.
La - dy, lis - ten to the rhy - thm of my

Em
Em6
Em
A7
Am
D
Am
D
Am
D
Am
D
rall. e dim.
heart - beat, And you'll get just what I mean.
rall. e dim.
Rhythmically
G
C♯dim
D7
Am11
fr3
Fm6
D7
Refrain:
Em - brace me, My sweet em - brace - a - ble you!
p - mf
Am
F7
D7
G
D7sus4
G
Em - brace me, You ir - re - place - a - ble you!

Em
Em7
Em6
F♯7
Bm
B♭+
Bm7
E7
Just one look at you, my heart grew tip - sy in me;
D
D♯°
A7
D7
You and you a - lone bring out the gyp - sy in me!
G
C♯°
D7
C
Fm6
D7
I love all the man - y charms a - bout you;

Am F7 D7 G7 D7sus4 Bbm6 G7 C
fr5
A-bove all I want my arms a-bout you. Don't be a
Am6 B7 Em Eb+ G Em6 G
naught-y ba-by, Come to pa-pa, Come to pa-pa, do! My sweet em-
L.H.
1. 2.
Cm6 D G Eb A D7 G
fr5
brace-a-ble you! you!

FIVE MINUTES MORE

Introduced to the public in the 1946 feature Sweetheart Of Sigma Chi *by Phil Brito, Frank Sinatra pounced on this great Sammy Cahn-Jule Styne creation and took it to the top of the charts, capturing the no. 1 spot for four weeks. Skitch Henderson, Frank's piano accompanist (and future* Tonight Show *band leader), released his own version, with a Ray Kellogg vocal, and joined Sinatra in the top-ten. Crowding the pop charts with other competing records were Tex Beneke, Bob Crosby, and the Three Suns—consisting of brothers Al and Morty Nevins on guitar and accordion and Artie Dunn on organ.*

Sinatra with director Richard Whorf, Cahn and Styne

Words by
SAMMY CAHN
Music by
JULE STYNE

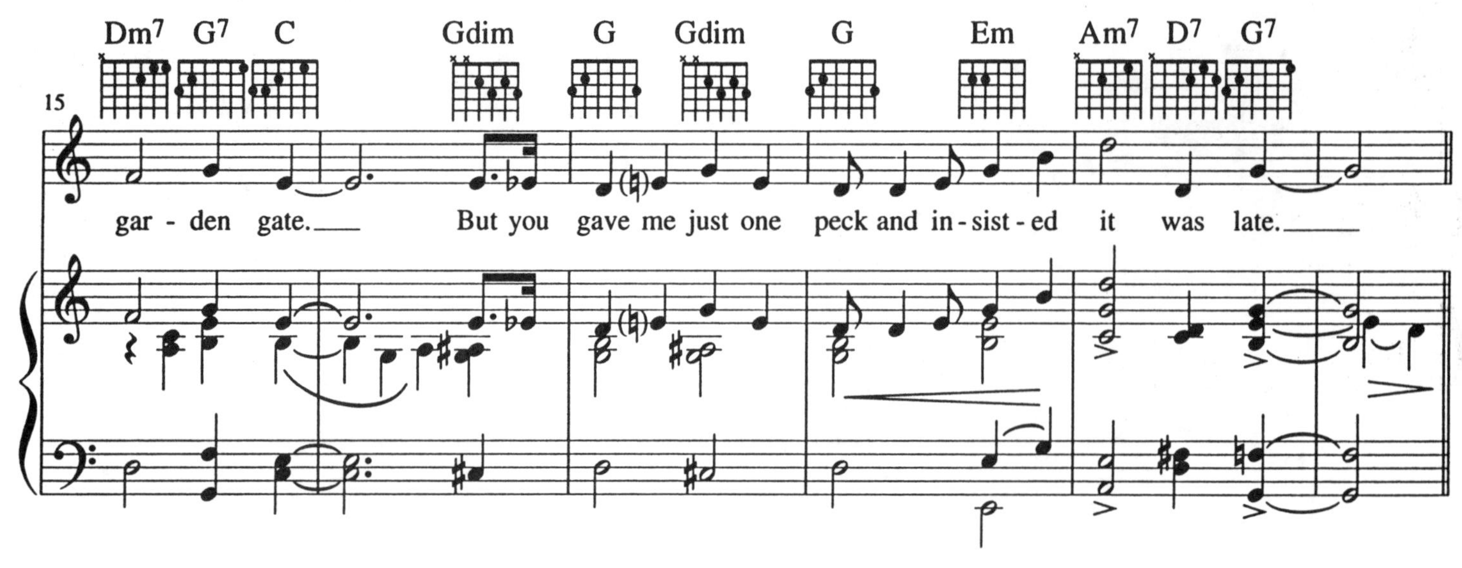
Dm7 G7 C Gdim G Gdim G Em Am7 D7 G7
15
gar - den gate. But you gave me just one peck and in - sist - ed it was late.

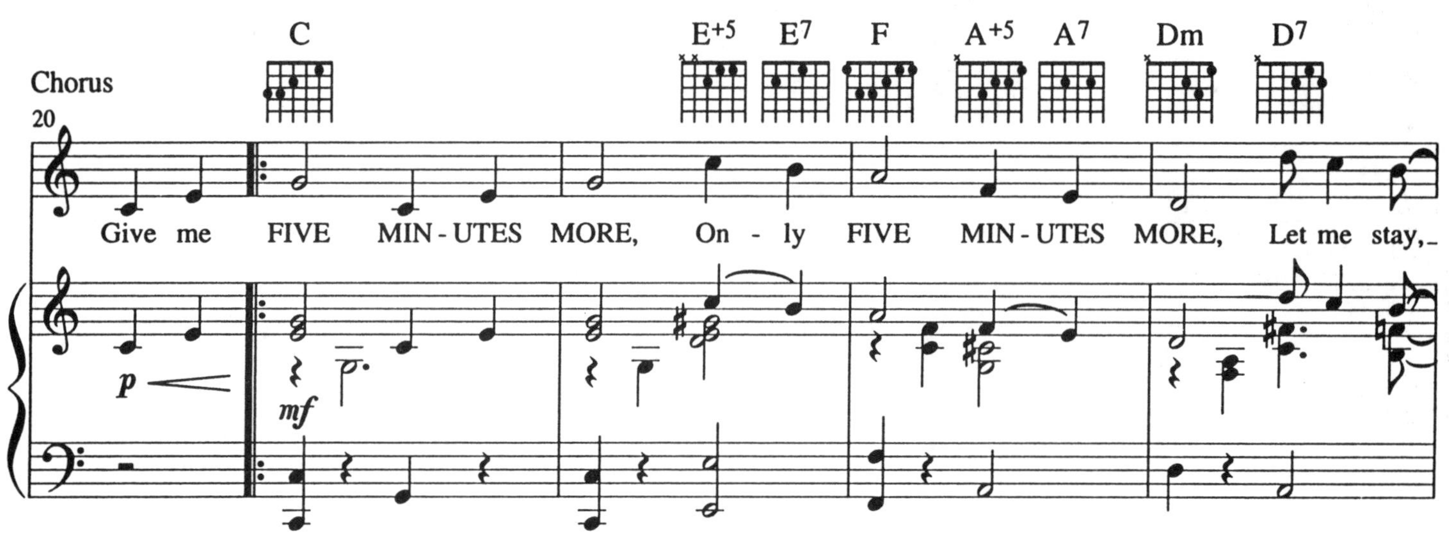
C E+5 E7 F A+5 A7 Dm D7
Chorus
20
Give me FIVE MIN - UTES MORE, On - ly FIVE MIN - UTES MORE, Let me stay,
p
mf

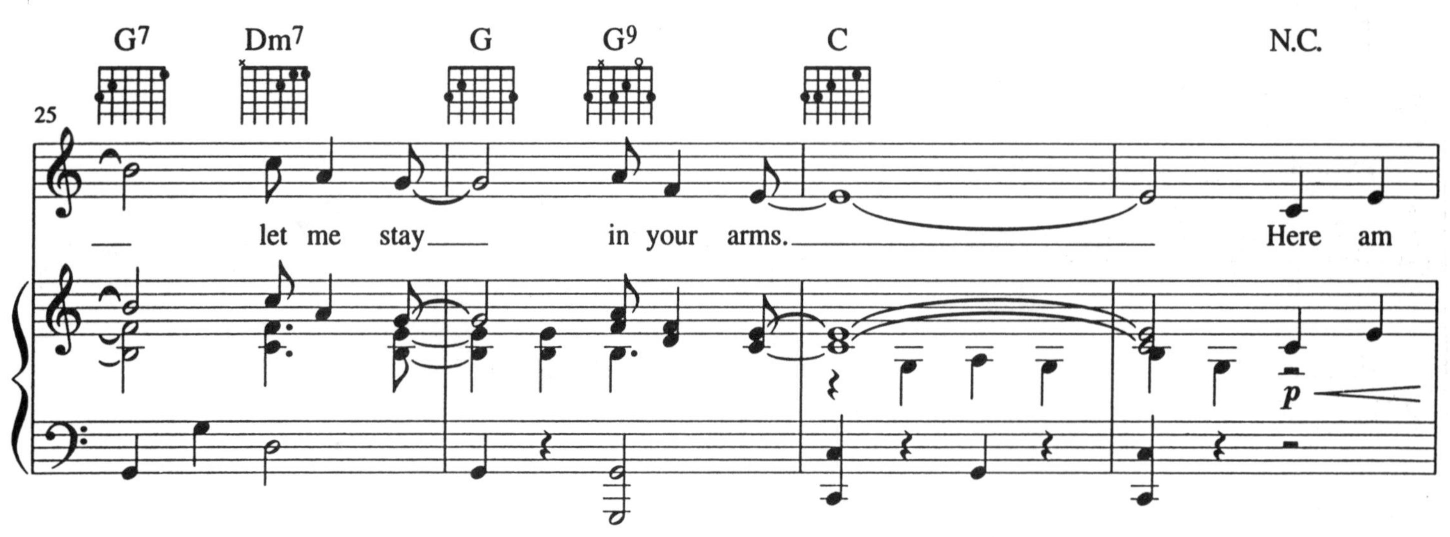
G7 Dm7 G G9 C N.C.
25
let me stay in your arms. Here am
p

C
E+5
E7
F
A+5
A7
Dm
D7
G7
Dm7
29
I beg-ging for On-ly FIVE MIN-UTES MORE, On-ly FIVE MIN-UTES MORE
mf
G7
G9
G7
C
Dm7
C
C+5
F
34
of your charms.
All week long I
f
Fm
C
Cdim
C
C
G7
Edim
C7
F
38
dreamed a-bout our Sat-ur-day date.
Don't you know that

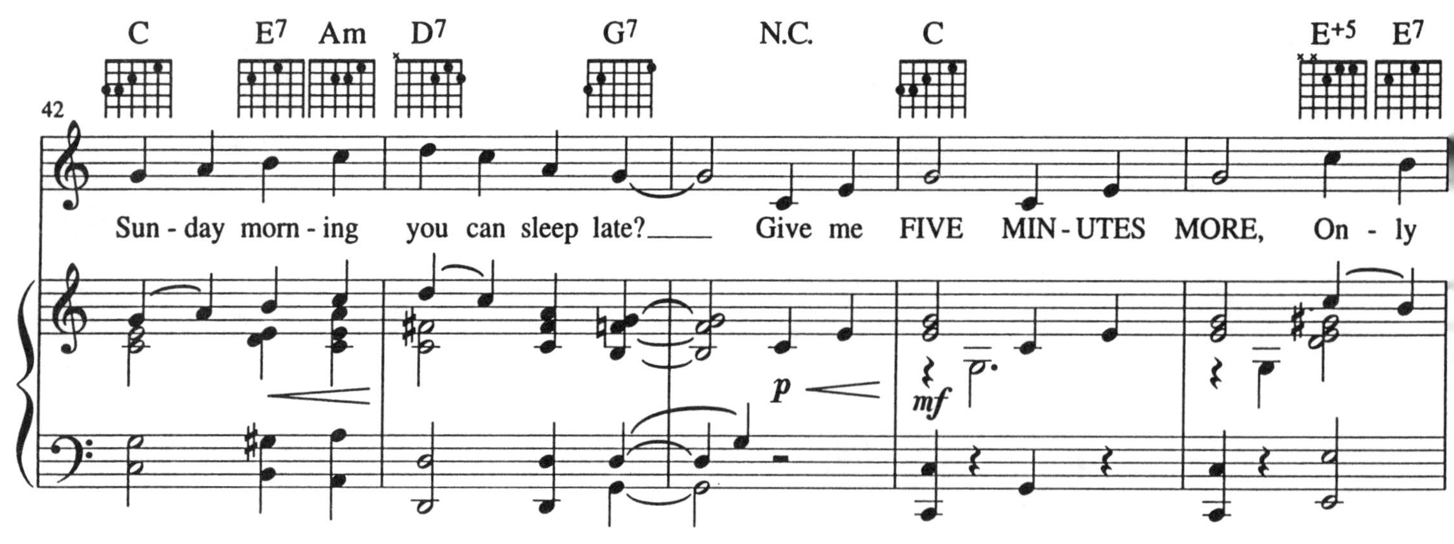
C
E7
Am
D7
G7
N.C.
C
E+5
E7
42
Sun - day morn - ing you can sleep late? Give me FIVE MIN - UTES MORE, On - ly
p
mf

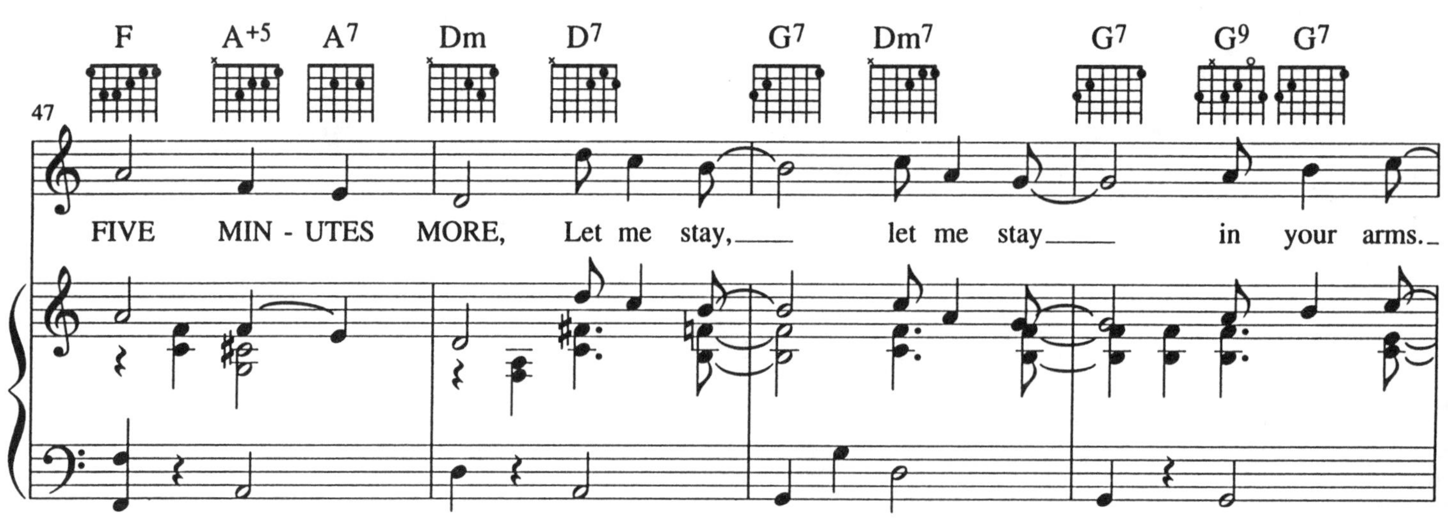
F
A+5
A7
Dm
D7
G7
Dm7
G7
G9
G7
47
FIVE MIN - UTES MORE, Let me stay, let me stay in your arms.

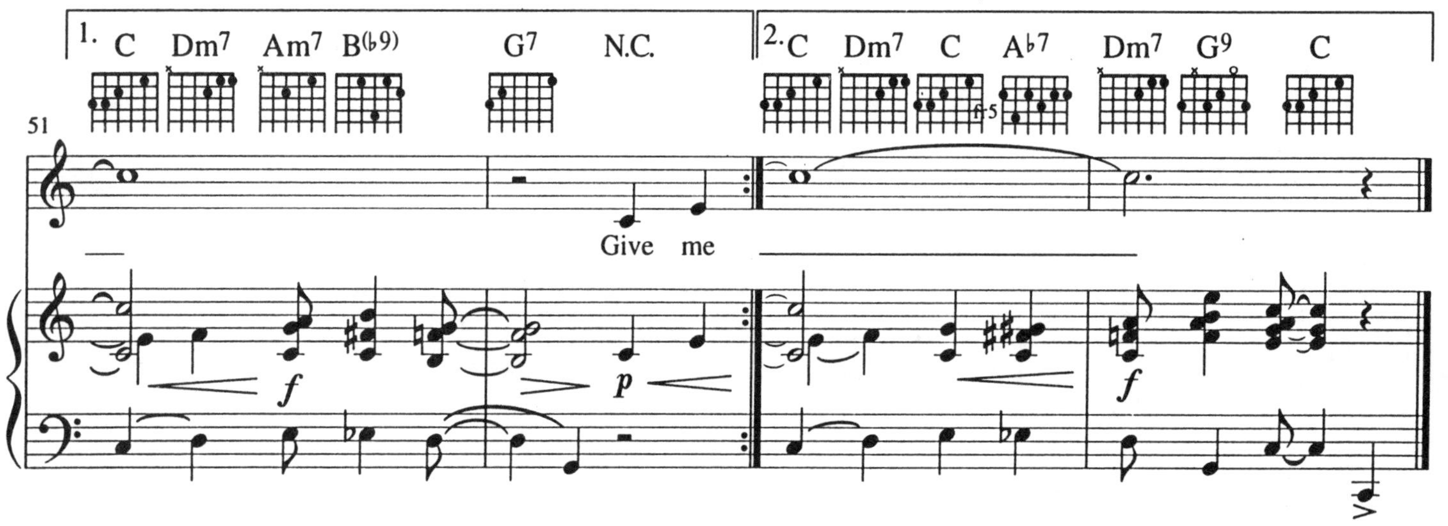
1. C
Dm7
Am7
B(♭9)
G7
N.C.
2. C
Dm7
C
A♭7
Dm7
G9
C
51
Give me
f
p

GET HAPPY

This "hallelujah" song made its first appearance in 1930's "Nine-Fifteen Revue," *where it shared the bill with numbers by Kay Swift, the Gershwins and Vincent Youmans. The revue closed after seven performances, but "Get Happy," memorably revived by Judy Garland in the 1950 film, "Summer Stock," is, very happily, with us still.*

Words and Music by
HAROLD ARLEN and
TED KOEHLER

Lively
Chorus:
Bb7
Eb6
Cm
3fr.
Eb
Ab/Bb
4fr.
Ebm
6fr.
Ab
Ab6
Eb7
For - get your troub - les and just get hap - py, you bet - ter
p - f
chase all your cares a - way. Sing Hal - le - lu - jah, come on, get
hap - py, get read - y for the judge - ment day. The sun is
shin - 'in, come on get hap - py, the Lord is wait - ing to take your hand.
Shout Hal - le - lu - jah! Come on, get hap - py, we're go -

Ab 4fr. Eb7 Ab6 4fr. Ab7 4fr. Db7 4fr.
ing to the prom - ised land. We're head - in' 'cross the Riv - er, wash your
fz fz
C7+5 F7/6 Bb7 Ab7 4fr. Db7 4fr. C7+5 F7/6
sins 'way in the tide. It's all so peace - ful on the oth - er
fz
dolce
Bb7 Eb Eb6 Bb7 Cm 3fr. Eb6 Bb7 Eb
side. For - get your troub - les and just get hap - py, you bet - ter
Eb6 Bb7 Cm 3fr. Ab/Bb 4fr. Eb Eb6 Bb7 Cm 3fr.
chase all your cares a way. Shout Hal - le - lu - jah! Come on, get
Eb6 Bb7 Ebm 6fr. Eb Bb7 1. Eb Cb7 Bb7 Eb 2. Eb
hap - py get read - y for the judge - ment day. For - get your day.

Anne Meara and Harry Guardino

FOR ALL WE KNOW

(From the Motion Picture "Lovers And Other Strangers")

A 1970 Oscar winner for Best Song, this melody could be heard in the film Lovers And Other Stangers. *The 1971 recording by the Carpenters was a million-seller earning a gold record.*

Words by
ROBB WILSON and ARTHUR JAMES
Music by
FRED KARLIN

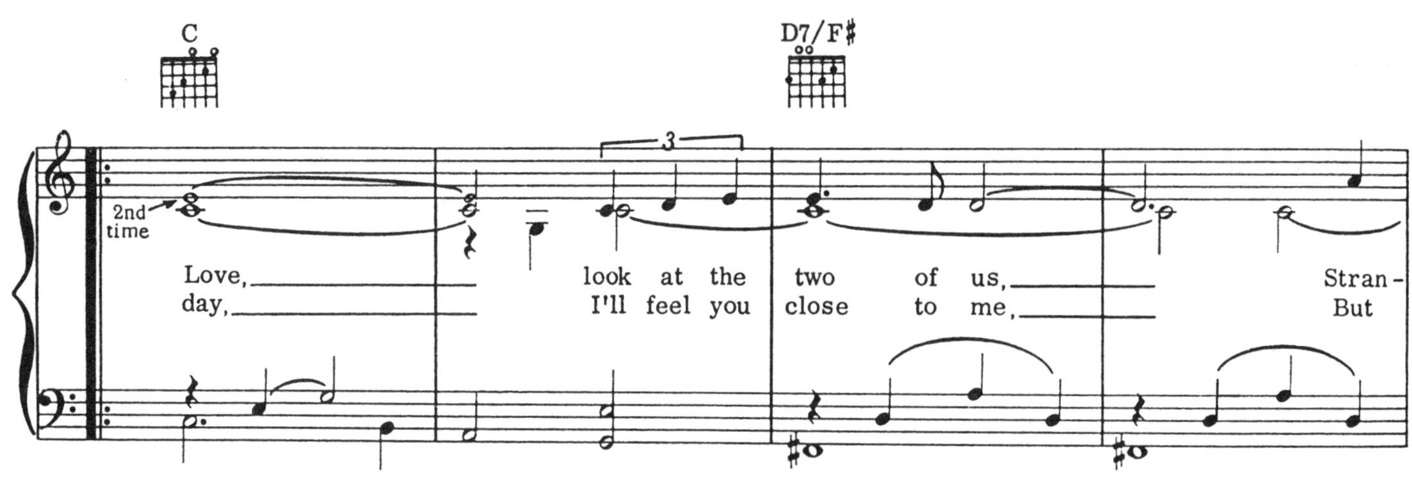

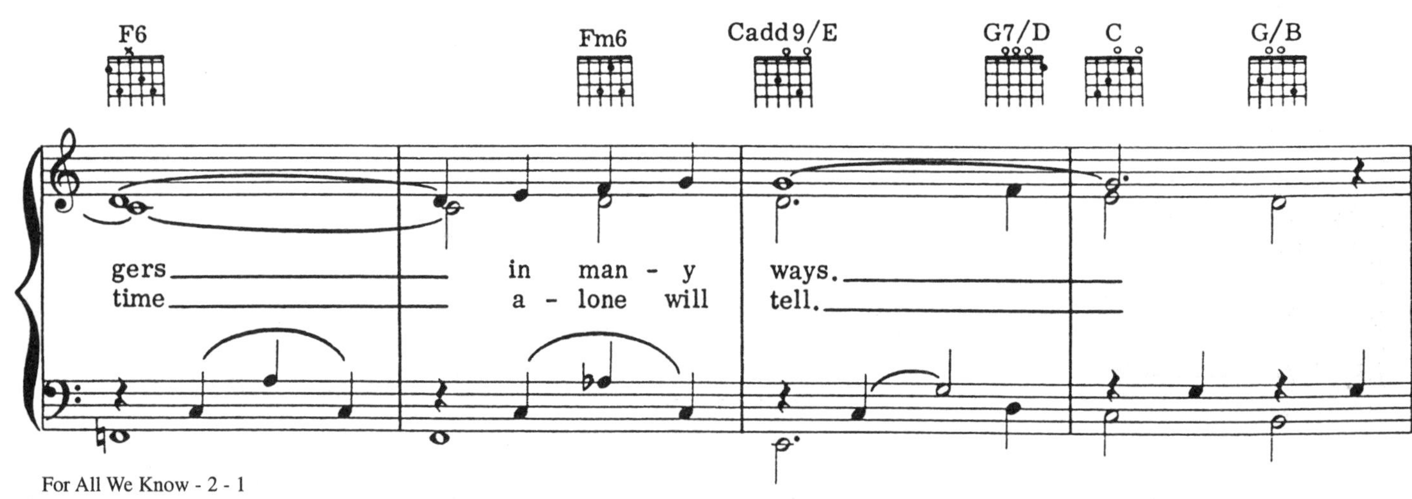

Am
Am/G
Am/F♯
D7
We've got a life - time to share, So much to
Let's take a life - time to say, "I knew you
Gmaj7
Cmaj7
Fmaj7
1. Dm7
Dm7/G
say And as we go from day to
well." For on - ly time
2. Dm7
Dm7/G
Em7
Am7
Fmaj7
will tell us so, And love may grow, For
3
3
Dm7/G
D7
D♭maj7
C6/9
All We Know.

GIGI

Sung by Louis Jourdan in the film of the same name. The song won the Academy Award as Best Song of 1958. Later used in the stage version of the musical in 1973.

Lyrics by
ALAN JAY LERNER

Music by
FREDERICK LOEWE

G G+ C6 Bdim Am7 D9 Dm7 F Gm7 G7 B
no! O - ver night there's been a breath - less change in you. Oh,
più espr.
dim.
p
C B F6 A7
Gi - gi, While you were tremb-ling on the brink, Was I out yon-der some-where blink-ing at a star? Oh,
Dm Dm7 Gm6 A7 Dm Dm7 F Fm6
Gi - gi, Have I been stand-ing up too close or back too far?
When did your spark - le turn to
espr.
C6 Em7 F6 Fm6 Cmaj7 C6 Fm C Em7 Edim
fi - re And your warmth be - come de - si - re? Oh, what mi - ra - cle has
Dm7 G7 C Dm7 Cmaj9
made you the way you are?

Tony Bennett

THE GOOD LIFE

Tony Bennett, the great singer who popularized such unforgettables as "Rags To Riches" and "I Left My Heart In San Francisco," once worked as a singing waiter! Although introduced by Kathy Keegan, "The Good Life," as performed by Mr. Bennett, became a huge Top Twenty smash in 1963.

Words by
JACK REARDON
Music by
SACHA DISTEL

Slowly, with feeling

mf

Ab Gm7

Oh, the good life full of fun seems to be the i - deal,

C7 Fm

Yes, the good life lets you hide all the sad - ness you

Dm7-5
G
Bbm7
feel, You won't real - ly fall in
Gb7
Ab
C7
love for you can't take the chance, So be
Fm
Bbm7
hon - est with your - self, don't try to fake ro - mance.

Eb7
Ab
It's the good life to be free and ex - plore the un -

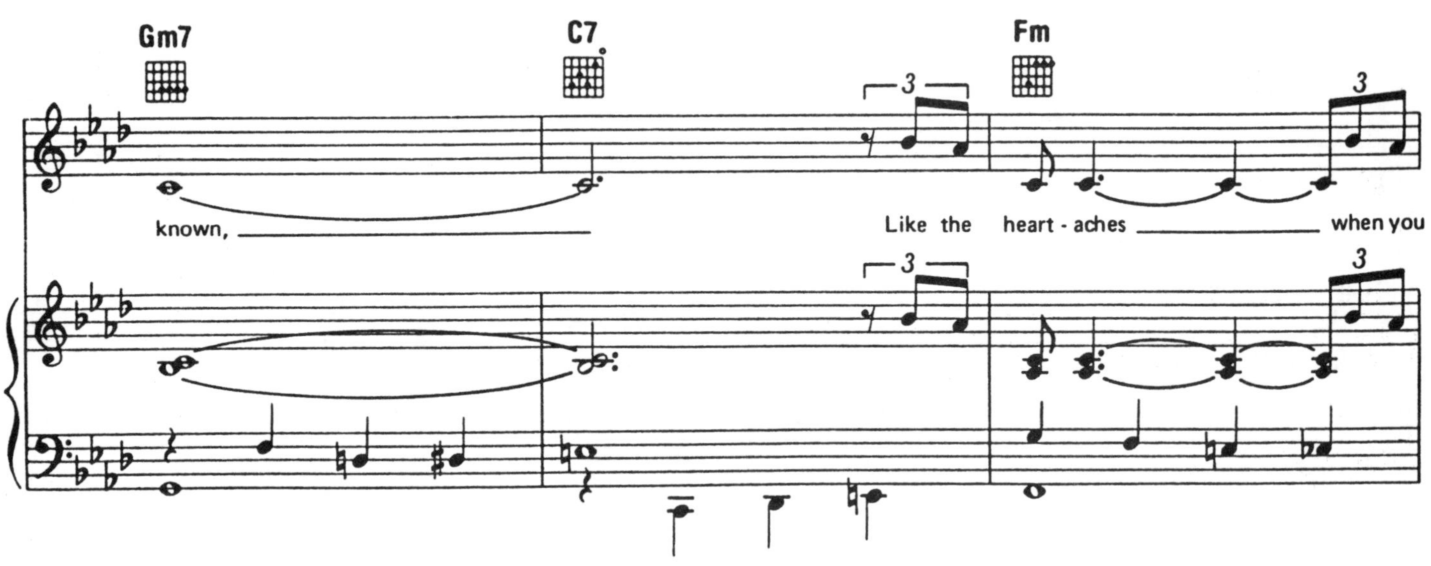
Gm7
C7
Fm
known,
Like the heart - aches when you

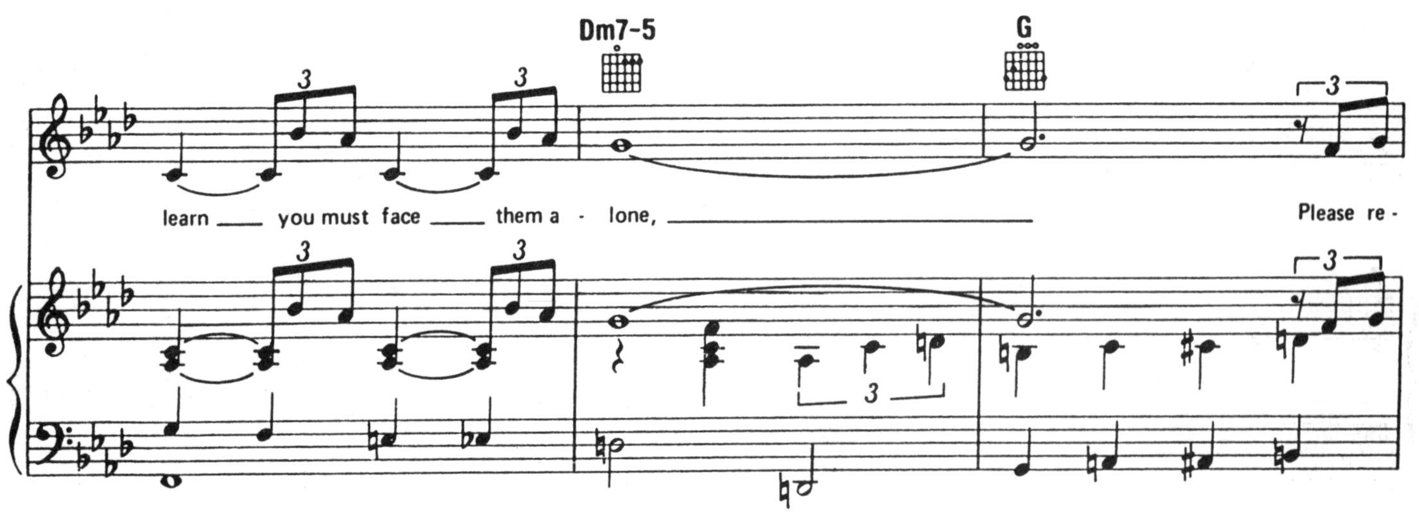
Dm7-5
G
learn you must face them a - lone,
Please re -

Bbm7
Gb7
Ab
mem - ber I still want you, and in case you won-der

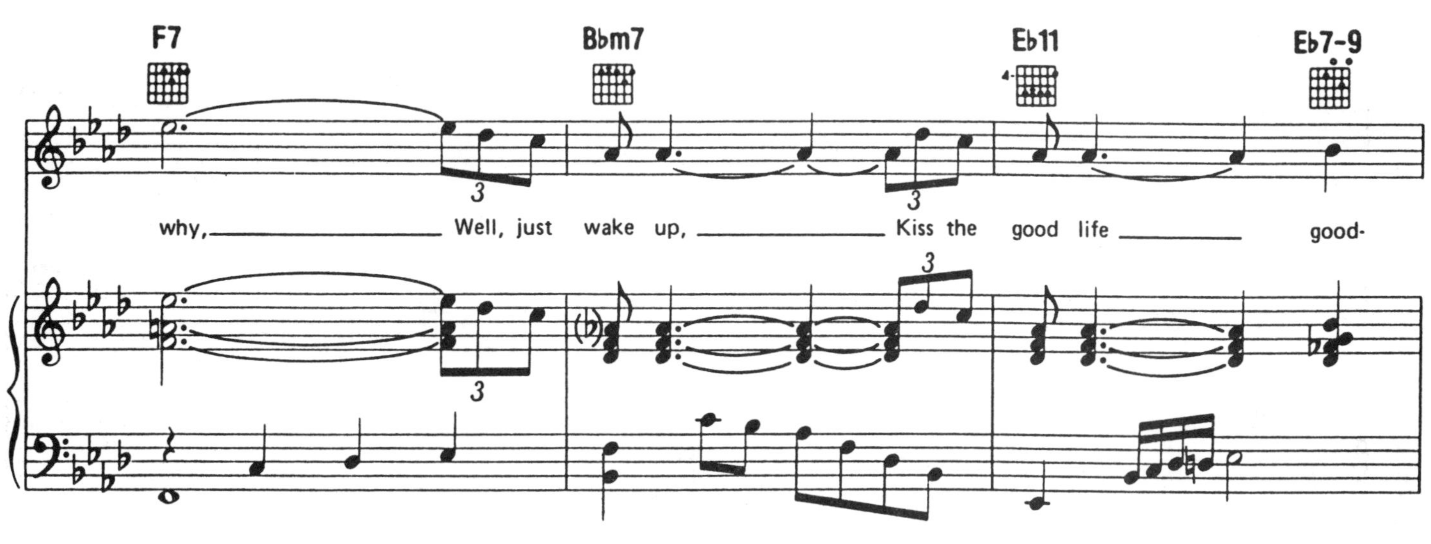
F7
Bbm7
Eb11
Eb7-9
why, Well, just wake up, Kiss the good life good-

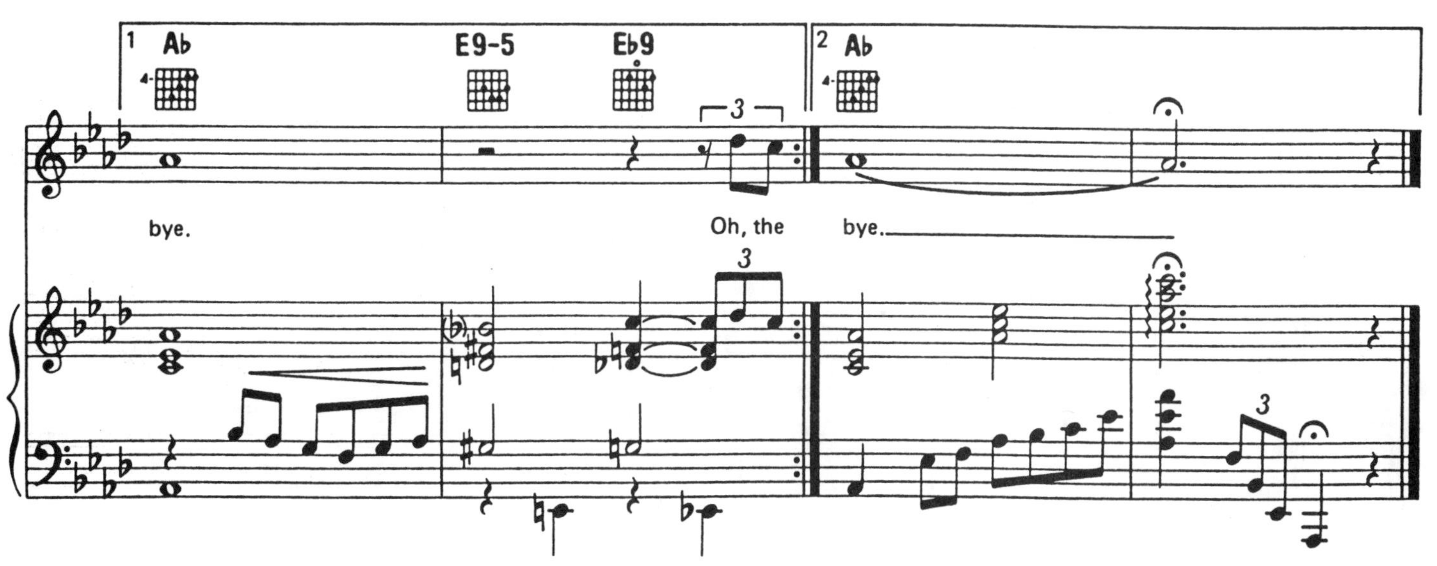
Ab
E9-5
Eb9
Ab
bye. Oh, the bye.

Judy Garland and Mickey Rooney

HOW ABOUT YOU?

Mickey Rooney and Judy Garland were the darlings of the silver screen when they performed this wonderful tune in the 1942 film, Babes On Broadway. *It was nominated for an Academy Award that year, and Tommy Dorsey's recording reached the top ten on the charts.*

Words by
RALPH FREED
Music by
BURTON LANE

Moderately

G Gmaj7 G B♭dim Am7 D7

mf I like New York in June, How A-bout You?

G Gmaj7 G F♯ Bm7-5 E7+5

I like a Gersh-win tune, How A-bout You?

A7 Cm6 D6 G6

I love a fire-side when a storm is due,

B B6 F♯7sus F♯7 B Am7 D7

I like po-ta-to chips, moon-light and mo-tor trips How A-bout You?

G Gmaj7 G B♭dim Am7 D7
I'm mad a - bout good books, can't get my fill,
G9 Dm7 G9 Dm7 Cmaj7 C6
And Frank - lin Roose - velt's looks, give me a thrill.
Cm G E♭7
Hold - ing hands in a mov - ie show, when all the lights are low
Am B7+5 B7 Em Em7 C D7
may not be new, But I like it, How A - bout
1. G Am7 D9
You?
2. G Am7 G
You?

Frank Sinatra

HIGH HOPES

"High Hopes," the Best Song Oscar-winner of 1959, was introduced in the movie A Hole In The Head *by Eddie Hodges and Frank Sinatra, for whom it was also a Top 40 chart hit.*

Words by
SAMMY CAHN

Music by
JAMES VAN HEUSEN

Moderato ***(with a beat)***

Piano

mf

Verse

F6 F♯o7

1. Next time you're found with your chin on the ground, There's a
2. When trou - bles call and your back's to the wall, There's a

mp

Gm7 3fr. C9 C6 C9 F Dm Gm7 3fr. C9

lot to be learned, So look a - round.
lot to be learned, That wall could fall.

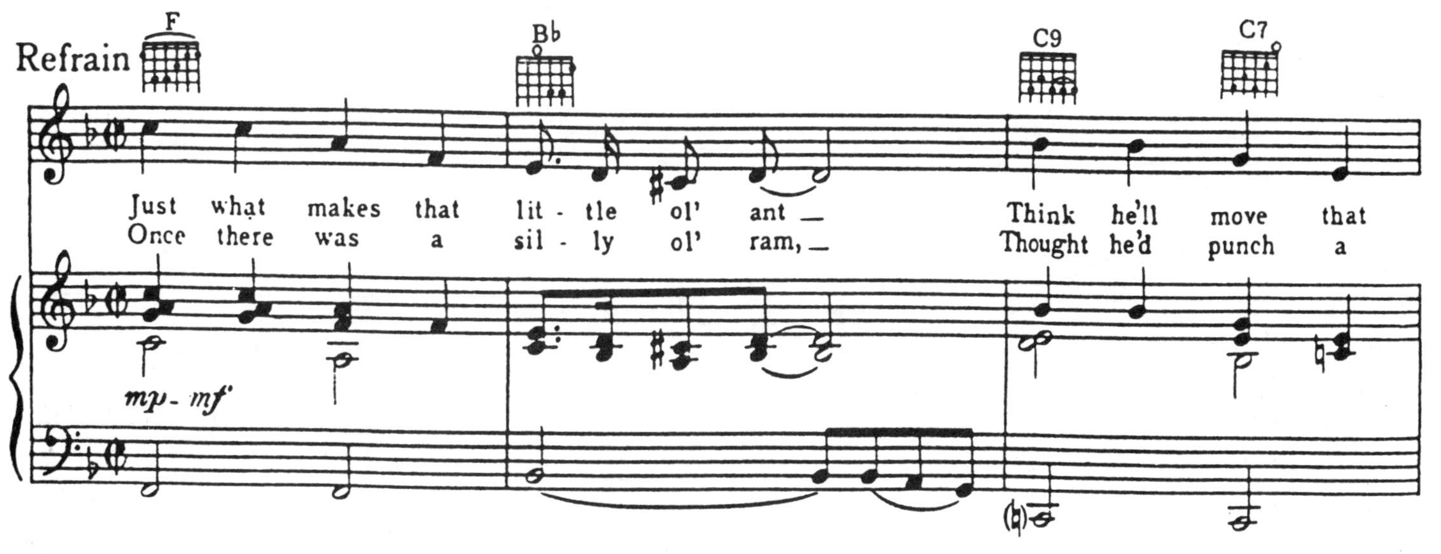
Refrain
F
B♭
C9
C7
Just what makes that lit - tle ol' ant _ Think he'll move that
Once there was a sil - ly ol' ram, _ Thought he'd punch a
mp - mf

F
F♯o7
Gm7
C♯o7
rub - ber tree plant; _ An - y - one knows _ an ant can't _
hole in a dam; _ No one could make _ that ram scram, _

Gm7
3fr.
C7
F
C7
F7
B♭
Bo7
Move a rub - ber tree plant. But he's got HIGH ___ HOPES, He's got
He kept but - tin' that dam. 'Cause he had HIGH ___ HOPES, He had
3. So keep your HIGH ___ HOPES, Keep your

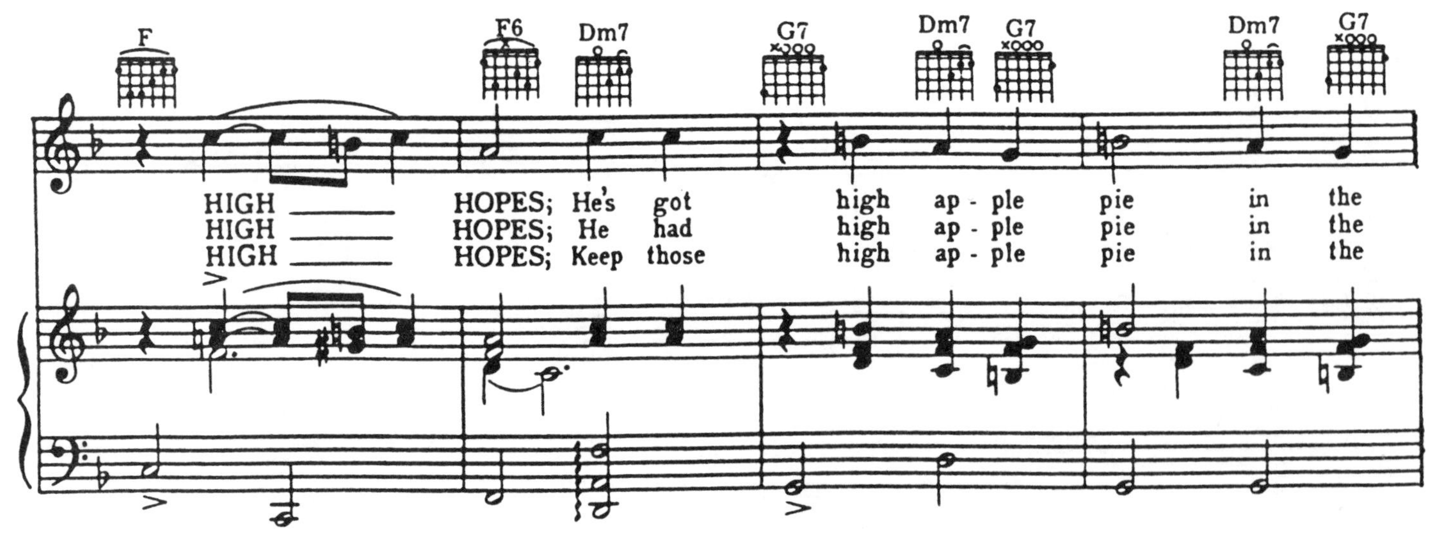
F
F6
Dm7
G7
Dm7
G7
Dm7
G7
HIGH HOPES; He's got high ap - ple pie in the
HIGH HOPES; He had high ap - ple pie in the
HIGH HOPES; Keep those high ap - ple pie in the

C7
F
sky hopes. So an - y time you're get tin' low,
sky hopes. So an - y time you're feel - in' bad,
sky hopes. A prob - lem's just a toy bal - loon,

F7
Bb
Bo7
'Stead of let - tin' go, Just re - mem - ber that ant.
'Stead of feel - in' sad, Just re - mem - ber that ram.
They'll be burst - ing soon, They're just bound to go "Pop!"

F6 F#o7 Gm7 3fr. C6 C9 F6 F#o7
Oops! There goes an - oth - er rub - ber tree plant. (Oops! There goes an -
Oops! There goes a bil - lion kil - o - watt dam. (Oops! There goes a
Oops! There goes an - oth - er prob - lem, ker - plop! (Oops! There goes an -
8va
Gm7 3fr. C7 F6 F#o7 Gm7 3fr. C6 C9
oth - er rub - ber tree plant) Oops! There goes an - oth - er rub - ber tree
bil - lion kil - o - watt dam) Oops! There goes a bil - lion kil - o - watt
oth - er prob - lem, ker - plop!) Oops! There goes an - oth - er prob - lem, ker -
8va
1. 2.
F F#o7 Gm7 3fr. C7
Back to Verse
plant!
dam!
3.
F C7 F
F6/9
plop! Ker plop!
3

Lucille Ball

HEY, LOOK ME OVER

Lucille Ball was the star attraction in the 1960 show Wildcat, *in which she and Paula Stewart performed this rouser. It was named to ASCAP's List of Hit Songs in 1960, and has become a trademark of political campaigns as well as colleges and universities.*

Music by
CY COLEMAN

Words by
CAROLYN LEIGH

March tempo
mf
sf
Refrain
G B7 F#m7 Ddim B7 E7
Hey, Look Me O - ver, lend me an ear; Fresh out of
mp - mf
(Opt.)
Am D7 Am7 Fm6 D7
clo - ver, mort-gaged up to here. But don't pass the plate, folks,
G B7 E7 A7
don't pass the cup; I fig-ure when-ev - er you're down and out, the

D7
G
B7
F#m7
only way is up. And I'll be up like a rose-bud, high on the
(Opt.)
Ddim
B7
E7
Am
vine; Don't thumb your nose, bud, take a tip from mine. I'm a
Cmaj7
F9
G
E7
lit-tle bit short of the el-bow room, but let me get me some,
1. And look
2. Hear me
Am7
D7
1.
G
2.
G
out, world, here I come.
shout,
come.

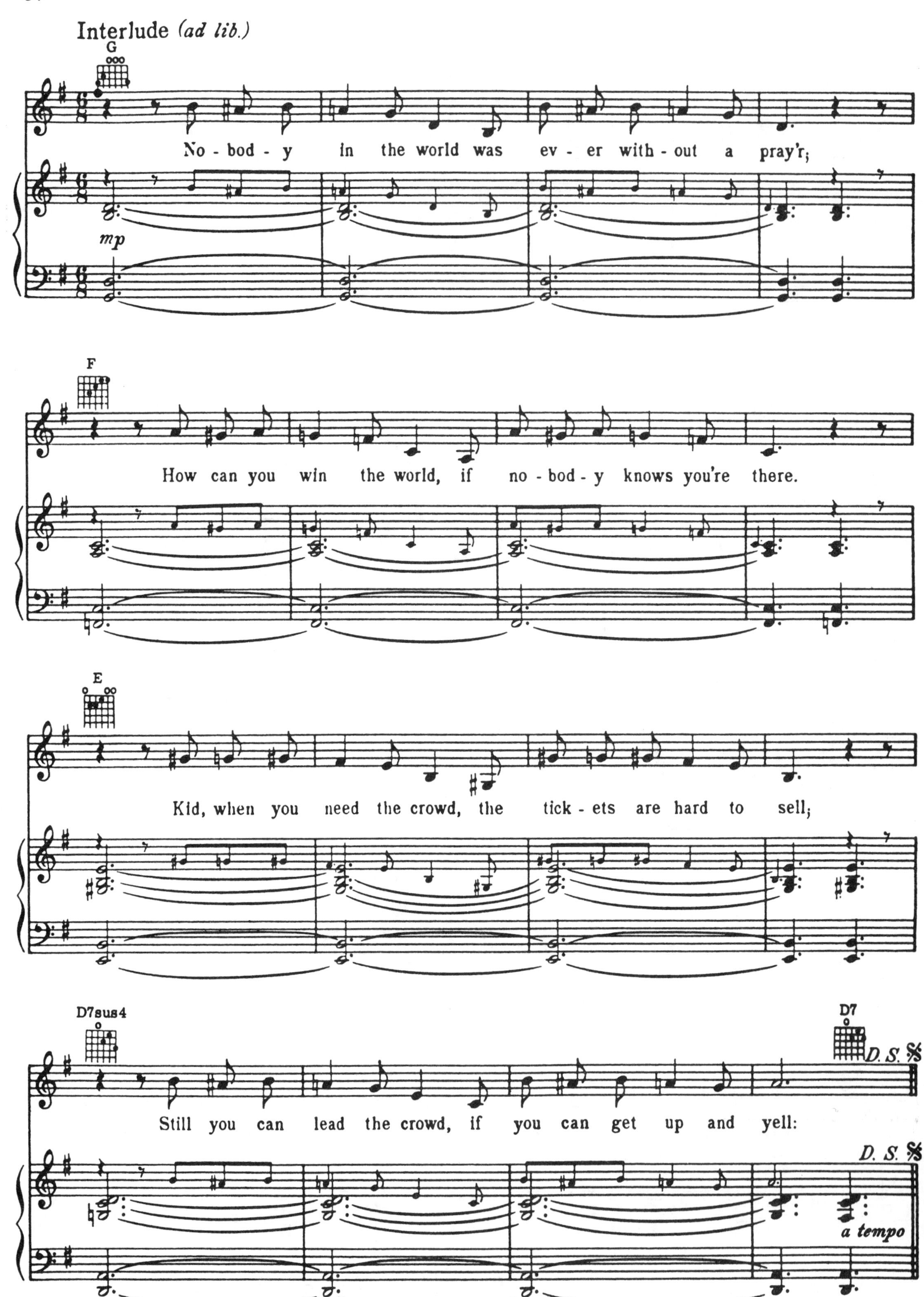
Interlude (ad lib.)
G
No - bod - y in the world was ev - er with - out a pray'r;
mp
F
How can you win the world, if no - bod - y knows you're there.
E
Kid, when you need the crowd, the tick - ets are hard to sell;
D7sus4
D7
D. S.
Still you can lead the crowd, if you can get up and yell:
D. S.
a tempo

HOW LITTLE WE KNOW
(How Little It Matters)

Nineteen fifty-six produced a few milestones in Frank Sinatra's career, including a rare collaboration with Der Bingle on the hit "Well Did You Evah?" (a song from the film High Society*) and yet another gold record to mount on the crowded walls of his home for "Hey! Jealous Lover." A favorite song of ours—and probably yours too—from that year is the hit "How Little We Know (How Little It Matters)," that was penned by Carolyn (Paula) Leigh ("Hey, Look Me Over," "I Won't Grow Up," "Witchcraft," "Young At Heart" and many others) and Philip Springer (the music critic, professor of electronic music, and composer for Broadway* [Ziegfeld Follies '57]*, film* [Summer Holiday]*, and TV* [Gunsmoke]*).*

Words by
CAROLYN LEIGH

Music by
PHILIP SPRINGER

F6
Am7
A♭m7
4fr.
Gm7
3fr.
C9
13
3
un - der - stand what touch - es off that tin - gle that sud - den ex -
F6
Dm
Am
A♭m7
4fr.
C7
17
plo - sion when two tin - gles in - ter - min - gle. Who cares to de -
Fmaj7
Gm7
3fr.
Am7
Dm7
Gm7
3fr.
G♭7
C7
21
fine what chem - is - try this is? Who cares with your

Fmaj7
Gm7
3fr.
Am7
Dm7
B♭m7
E♭9
25
3
lips on mine how ig - nor - ant bliss is? So long as you
Cm7
3fr.
F9
F7-9
Dm7
E♭9
Dm7
29
kiss me and the world a - round us shat - ters. How lit - tle it mat - ters.
1.
2.
Gm7
3fr.
C7-9
F6
Gm7
3fr.
C
F6
C9
F6
34
How lit - tle we know. How lit - tle we know.

Frankie Laine

I BELIEVE

Jane Froman, one of America's favorite Broadway, radio and television personalities of the '30s, '40s and '50s, introduced this anthem of faith in 1953 on her television show U.S.A. Canteen. *Frankie Laine's recording that same year reached no. 2 on the pop charts and was certified gold.*

Words and Music by
ERVIN DRAKE, IRVIN GRAHAM,
JIMMY SHIRL and AL STILLMAN

Moderately ***(with much expression)***

f

C Am Dm G7 Dm7 G7 C

I BE-LIEVE for ev-'ry drop of rain that falls, a flow-er grows.

p-mf

Dm7 G7-9 C C+ Am Dm G7

I BE-LIEVE that some-where in the dark-est night, a can-dle

C
Cmaj7
C6
C
Am7
Em
F
glows.
I BE-LIEVE for ev - 'ry-one who goes a - stray,
B7
E
Emaj7
E7
E7-9
Am
Am7
some-one will come to show the way.
Dm7
G9
G7
Dm7
G7
C
Am
I BE - LIEVE, I BE- LIEVE.
I BE-LIEVE a - bove the storm the
Dm
G7
Dm7
G7
C
Dm7
G7-9
C
C+
Am
small- est pray'r will still be heard.
I BE-LIEVE that some-one in the

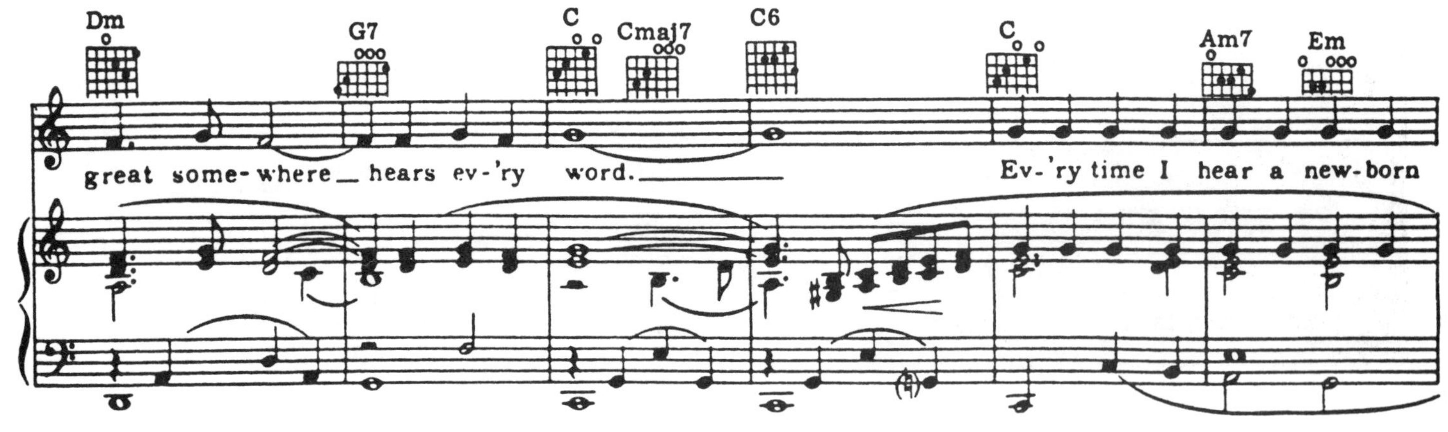
Dm
G7
C
Cmaj7
C6
C
Am7
Em
great some-where hears ev-'ry word.
Ev-'ry time I hear a new-born

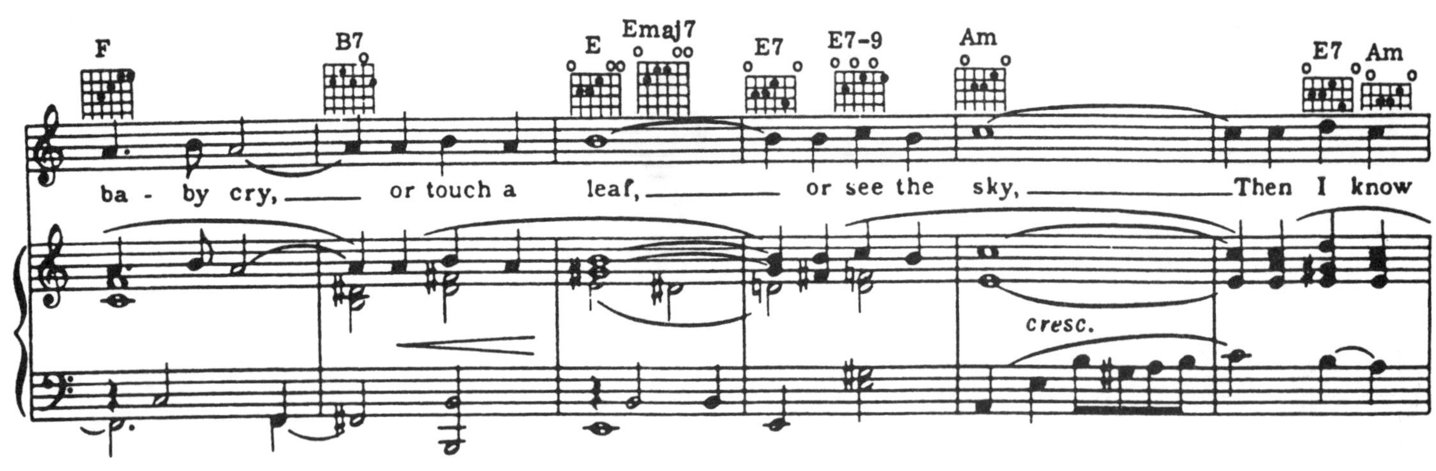
F
B7
E
Emaj7
E7
E7-9
Am
E7
Am
ba - by cry, or touch a leaf, or see the sky, Then I know
cresc.

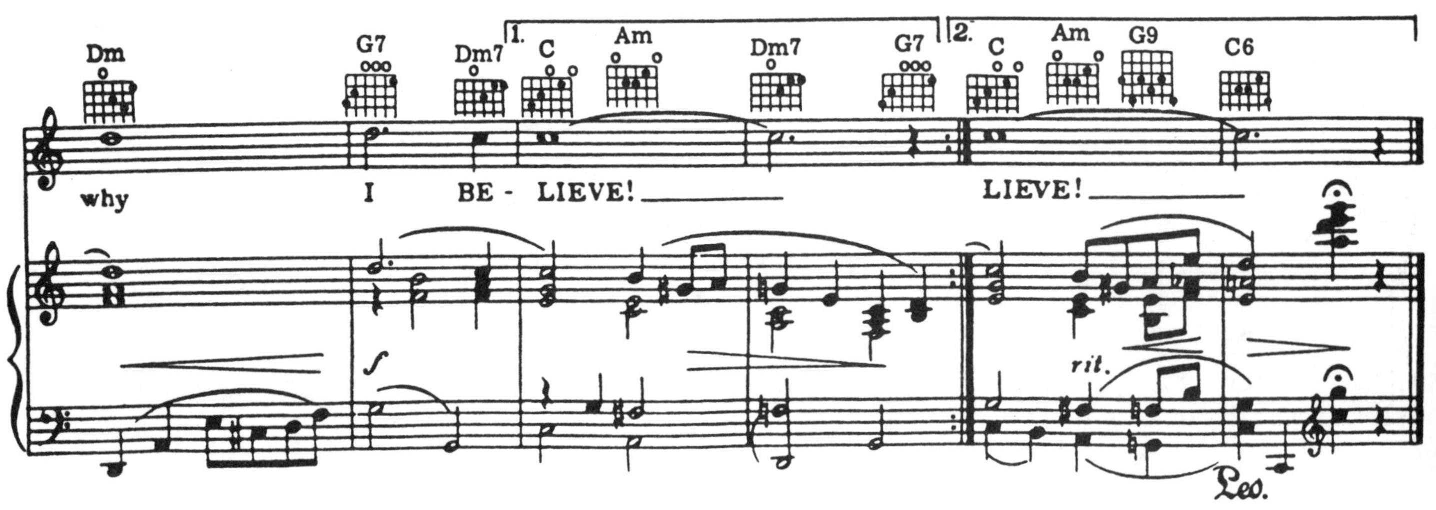
Dm
G7
Dm7
1.
C
Am
Dm7
G7
2.
C
Am
G9
C6
why I BE - LIEVE!
LIEVE!
rit.

I DIDN'T KNOW WHAT TIME IT WAS

Introduced in the 1939 stage musical Too Many Girls, *"I Didn't Know What Time It Was" has since burrowed a niche in nearly every major artist's repertoire. James Taylor's contemporary interpretation is available on the soundtrack of the 1992 boxoffice smash* A League Of Their Own, *starring Geena Davis, Tom Hanks and Madonna.*

Words by
LORENZ HART
Music by
RICHARD RODGERS

Am Dm7 D7 F♯m7 B7 Em F♯m7 B7
too! I did - n't know what day it was. You held my
A Am Em Bm C Bm
hand, Warm like the month of May it was And I'll say it was
Am7 Dm7 D7 G Am B7 Am B7
grand. Grand to be a - live, to be young, to be mad, to be yours a -
mf piu espr.
Em C D7 G
lone! Grand to see your face, feel your touch hear your

A7
Am7
Dm7
D7
F#m7
B7
Em
voice say I'm all your own!
I didn-n't know what year it was.
p
F#m7
B7
A
Am
Em
Bm
Life was no prize.
I want-ed love and here it was
C
Bm
Am7
Am7-5
G
B7
C6
D
C
Shin-ing out of our eyes. I'm wise and I know what time it is
1.
G
C#m7-5
D7
2.
G
G6
now!
mf
now!
f
8 bassa

Kathryn Grayson, Frank Sinatra and Gene Kelly

I FALL IN LOVE TOO EASILY

This 1945 Academy Award nominee for Best Song was performed by Frank Sinatra in the Oscar winning film Anchors Aweigh, *also starring Gene Kelly and Kathryn Grayson. By this time, Sammy Cahn and Jule Styne had become Frank Sinatra's personal songwriting team, as represented on the recent mini-series,* The Sinatra Story.

Words by
SAMMY CAHN

Music by
JULE STYNE

Moderately

mf

Fm7 B♭9 E♭ (fr5)

mp

There are those who can leave love or take it______ Love to

Fm7 B♭7 D E♭ (fr5) B♭ Cm7 F7

them is just what they make it______ I wish that I were the

B♭ A7 B♭ G7 Cm7 F7 Fm7 B♭7

same______ But love is my fav - 'rite game.

Slowly (with feeling)

Chorus

Fm7 B♭7 E♭ Fm6 G7aug Cm

mp I Fall In Love Too Eas - i - ly, I fall in love too fast,

Fm G7aug Cm Cm7 D7 D7-5 Fm6 G7 G9♭

I fall in love too ter - ri - bly hard, For love to ev - er last.

Cm7 D7 G7 C Dm7 C C7 Fm B♭m E♭9

My heart should be well schooled 'Cause I've been fooled in the past, And still I

Fm7 B♭7 E♭ E♭7 A♭ B♭-9 1. E♭ B♭-9+5 E♭ Cm7 2. E♭

Fall In Love Too Eas - i - ly I fall in love too fast. fast.

Fred Astaire

I GUESS I'LL HAVE TO CHANGE MY PLAN

The Original lyric to this melody was written in 1924 by Lorenz Hart when he and Arthur Schwartz were summer camp counselors, and it was titled "I Love To Lie Awake In Bed." In 1929, with a new lyric by Howard Dietz, it was introduced in the Broadway production The Little Show. *In what is now considered a classic, Fred Astaire and Jack Buchanan performed a top hat and white tie duo to this tune in the 1953 film* The Band Wagon.

Words by
HOWARD DIETZ

Music by
ARTHUR SCHWARTZ

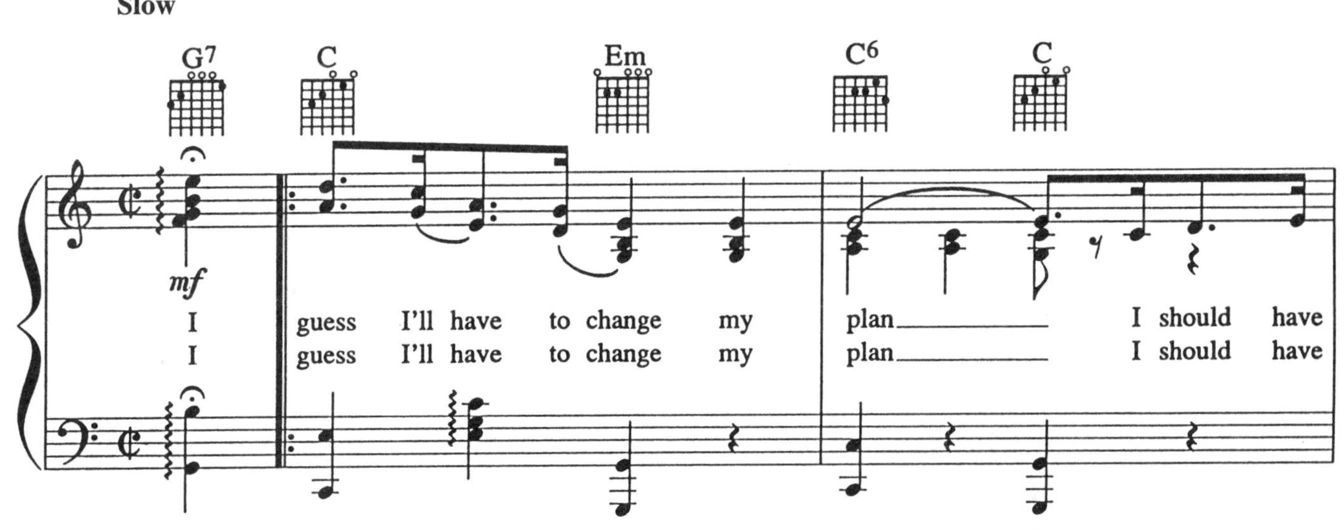

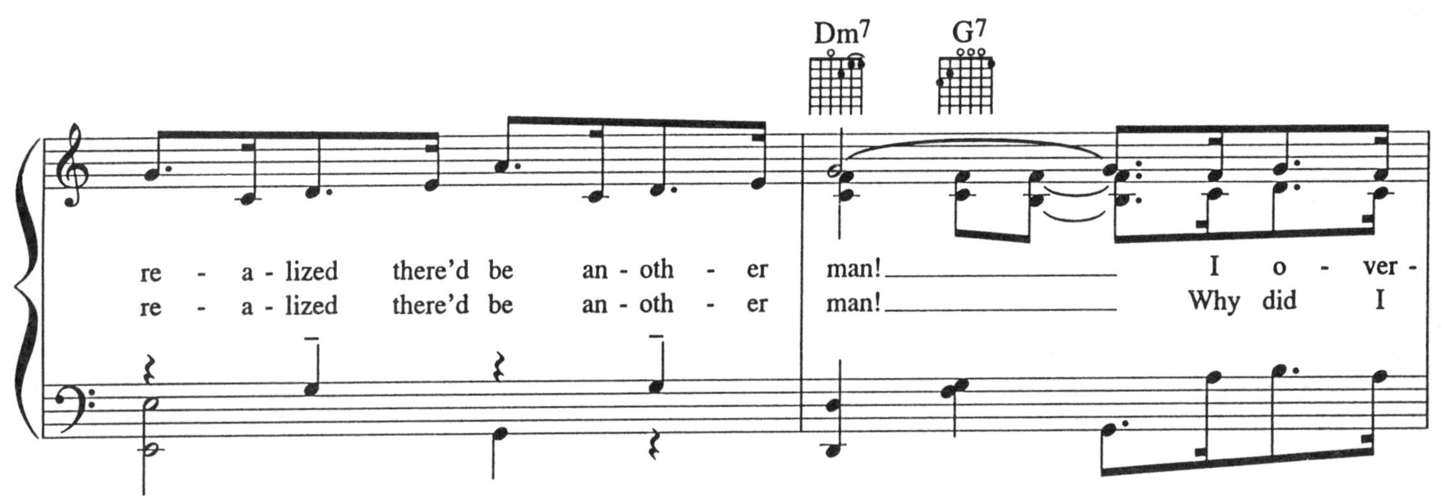

Em F♯7 Fmaj7 G7 C G+

looked that point com - plete - ly______ Un - til the
buy those blue pa - ja - mas______ Be - fore the

Am7 Am7-5 D7 Dm7 Dm7-5 G7

big af - fair be - gan; Be -
big af - fair be - gan? My

C Em C6 C

fore I knew where I was at______ I found my -
boil - ing point is much too low______ For me to

C7 F

self up - on the shelf, and that was that______ I tried to
try to be a sly Lo - tha - ri - o!______ I think I'll

F6
Fm6
C
reach the moon but when I got there,
crawl right back and in - to my shell,
Em
B
G7
Gdim
G7
All that I could get was the air, My
Dwell - ing in my per - son - al hell. I'll
C
Em
C6
C
feet are back up - on the ground I've lost the
have to change my plan a - round I've lost the
Dm7
G7
1.
C
G7
C
G7
2.
C
one girl I found. I
one girl I found.
sf

Donna Reed and Steve Allen in
The Benny Goodman Story

I THOUGHT ABOUT YOU

The 1939 collaboration between Van Heusen and Mercer brought forth this haunting melody, one which lends itself to improvisation. Hence, it has become a jazz standard. Berry Goodman successfully recorded it in 1940.

Words by
JOHNNY MERCER
Music by
JIMMY VAN HEUSEN

Moderato

mf

Eb D7 G7+5/Db C9+5 C9 F9 Cm7 F7

Refrain *(Slowly and Rhythmically)*

I took a trip on the train and I THOUGHT A-BOUT YOU,

p-mf

Fm7 Gm/Bb G7 Cm Bbm7 Eb7sus Cm Eb7

I passed a shad-ow-y lane and I THOUGHT A-BOUT YOU,

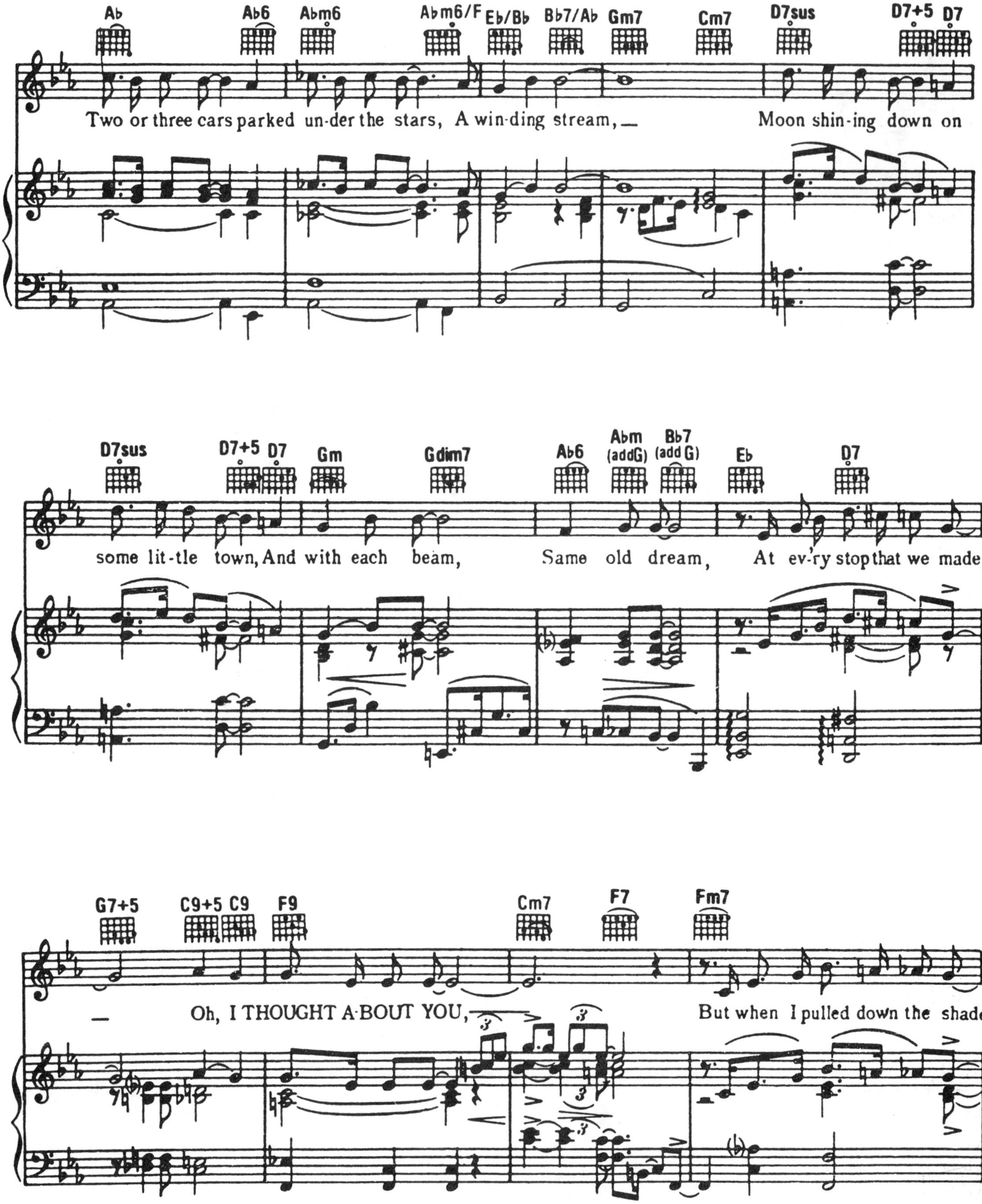

Ab Ab6 Abm6 Abm6/F Eb/Bb Bb7/Ab Gm7 Cm7 D7sus D7+5 D7
Two or three cars parked un-der the stars, A win-ding stream, — Moon shin-ing down on
D7sus D7+5 D7 Gm Gdim7 Ab6 Abm (addG) Bb7 (add G) Eb D7
some lit-tle town, And with each beam, Same old dream, At ev-'ry stop that we made,—
G7+5 C9+5 C9 F9 Cm7 F7 Fm7
— Oh, I THOUGHT A-BOUT YOU, But when I pulled down the shade,

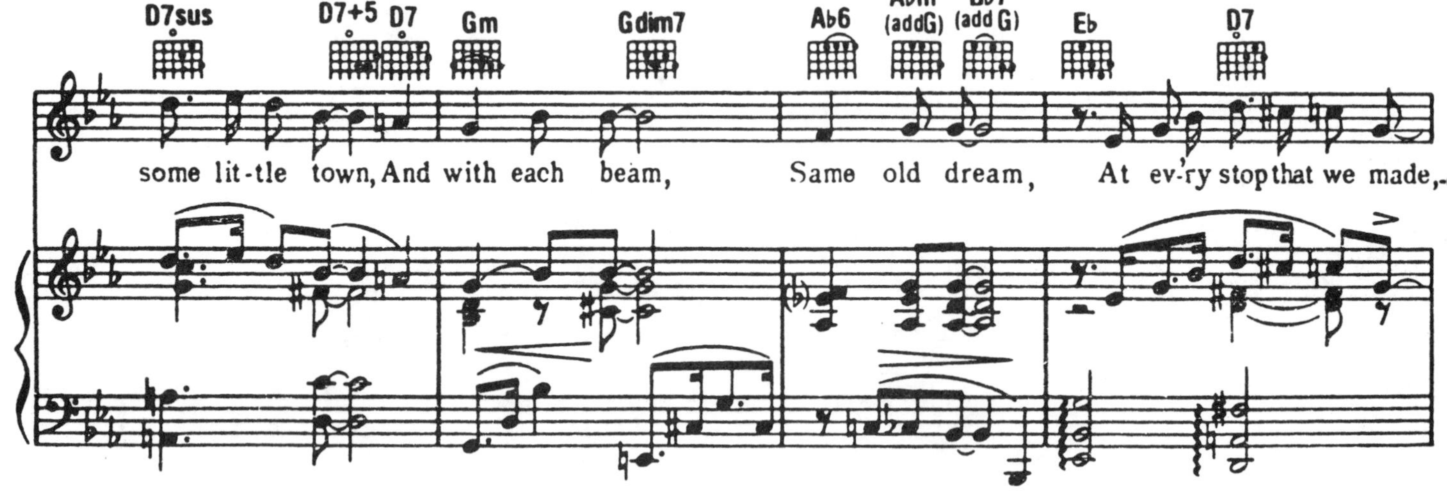

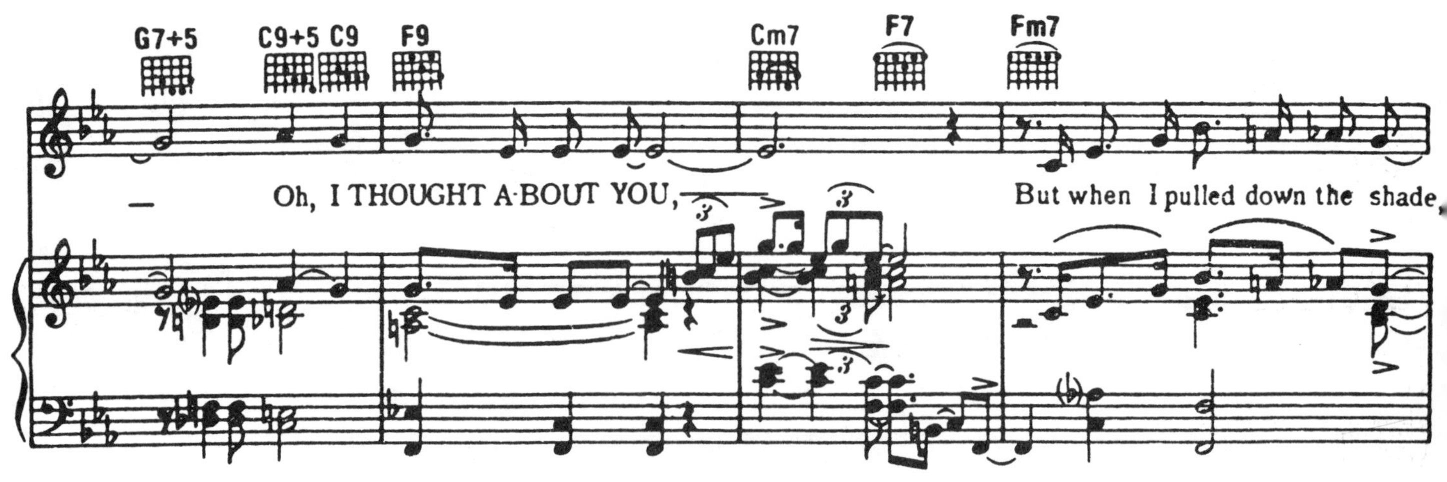

Gm/Bb
G7
Cm
Bbm7
Eb7sus
Eb7
Ab
Ab6
— then I real - ly felt blue, I peeked thru the crack and
Abm6
Abm6/F
Eb
Eb6
Ab7
F13
F#dim7
Fm7
Bb7 (add G)
Bb7
looked at the track, The one go-ing back to you, And what did I do?
Fm7
Bb13-9
1
Eb6
Cm
Fm7
Bb7
2
Eb6
E7(#9)
Eb6/9
I THOUGHT A-BOUT YOU!
poco rit.

Benny Goodman

I WANT TO BE HAPPY

No, No, Nanette *is an all-time favorite Vincent Youmans show. With two Broadway productions (1924 and 1971) that were the biggest hits of their respective seasons and two popular film versions in 1930 and 1940 (not to forget 1950's* Tea For Two*), it should come as quite a surprise that the show almost closed during previews in Detroit. The pre-Broadway try-out was panned by critics and audiences alike. Instead of capitulating, the producers revised the show and, most importantly, added two new tunes. The new songs, with music by Youmans and lyrics by Irving Caesar turned out to be the outstanding hits of the show which, itself, proved a triumph. The songs, "Tea For Two" and "I Want To Be Happy" quickly entered the pop-standards repertoire. "I Want To Be Happy" entered the charts many times with hit records by Carl Fenton, Vincent Lopez, Jan Garber, and the Shannon Four in the 1924-25 season alone. Later successes included versions by Red Nichols and His Five Pennies (1930), Benny Goodman (1937), the Tommy Dorsey Orchestra Starring Warren Covington (1958; after Tommy's death), Enoch Light and the Light Brigade (1958) and Lena Horne (1981).*

Lyrics by
IRVING CAESAR

Music by
VINCENT YOUMANS

Moderato

C Dm7 G7 C Dm7 G7

James: I'm a ver-y or-di-nar-y man, try-ing to work out life's hap-py plan,
Nanette: No one ev-er talked like that to me, I have nev-er known such sym-pa-thy,

C Cdim G7sus4 Dm7 G7 C

do-ing un-to oth-ers as I'd like to have them do-ing un-to me.
on-ly in my dreams, it real-ly seems to me it's too good to be true.

Em
C♯m7(♭5)
B7
Em
D♯+5
G6
A9
A9(♭5)
fr3
13
When I find a ver - y lone - ly soul, to be kind be - comes my on - ly goal,
There are smil - ing fac - es ev - 'ry where, sure - ly I de - serve my lit - tle share,
G
C
G
Gdim
D7
G7
G°7
G7
Gmaj7+5
17
I feel so much bet - ter when I tell them my phil - os - o - phy.
I'm a luck - y girl to know that I can get it all from you.
C
Dm7/G
G7
Dm7/G
21
p – f
I want to be hap - py, but I won't
G7
Dm7/G
G7
Dm7/G
G7
Dm7/G
G7
Dm7/G
G7
24
be hap - py till I make you hap - py,

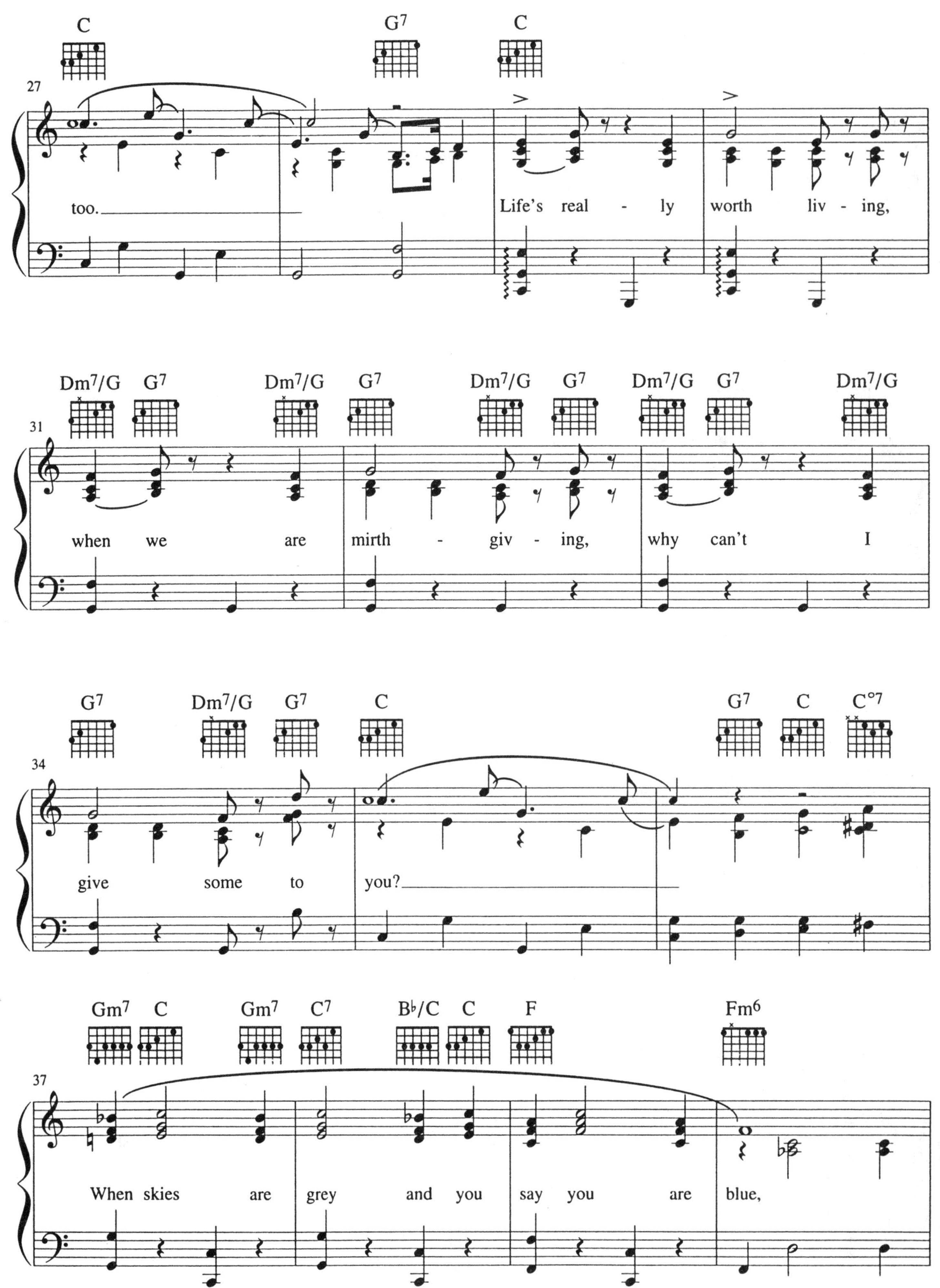
C G7 C
27
too.
Life's real - ly worth liv - ing,
Dm7/G G7 Dm7/G G7 Dm7/G G7 Dm7/G G7 Dm7/G
31
when we are mirth - giv - ing, why can't I
G7 Dm7/G G7 C G7 C C°7
34
give some to you?
Gm7 C Gm7 C7 B♭/C C F Fm6
37
When skies are grey and you say you are blue,

C
C6
Dm7
G7
41
I'll send the sun smil - ing through.
45
Dm7/G
I want to be hap - py, but I won't
48
be hap - py till I make you hap - py,
1.
2.
51
too.
f
too.
f
8va
ffz

Dick Haymes and Harry James

I'LL GET BY
(As Long As I Have You)

Fred Ahlert was one of the most talented and most prolific composers of the century; Roy Turk one of the truly great lyricists. Published in 1928, this evergreen enjoyed sheet music sales and record sales of over a million copies each. It was revived in 1944 with a no. 1 recording by the Harry James orchestra with Dick Haymes on vocal, and in 1961 vocalist Shirley Bassey had a successful recording. It was included in a half dozen films from 1930 to 1957.

Words by
ROY TURK

Music by
FRED E. AHLERT

Moderately

mf

C6 Ddim C6 G7-9 C6 Bm7 E7 E7+5 Dm

I'll Get By as long as I have you.

mp

Edim Dm7 Am7 D9 Bm G7sus4 G7 E♭dim

Tho' there be rain and dark-ness too, I'll

G7
G9
G7
G7+5
C
Em6
C♯dim
Dm7
G9
C6
Ddim
C6
not com - plain,
I'll
see it
through.
Pov - er - ty
G7
C
Bm7
E7
E7+5
Dm
A7-9
may
come to
me,
that's
true,
But
Dm7
E7+5
E7
E7-9
Am
Em7
A9
A7+5
Dm7
what care I,
say,
I'll Get
By
as
long as
I
G7-9
1. C6
Am7
Dm7
G7
2. C6
A♭maj7
A♭6
D♭9
C9/6
have
you.
you.

Doris Day and Danny Thomas

I'LL SEE YOU IN MY DREAMS

Jeanette MacDonald sang it in Follow The Boys, *Bob Crosby in* Pardon My Rhythm, *Jean Crane hummed it in* Margie... *not to tamper with greatness, but might we suggest "I'll See You In The Movies" as an alternate title? It was even used as the title song (in a Doris Day performance) for the film biography of Gus Kahn.*

Words by GUS KAHN
Music by ISHAM JONES

Moderately

mf *rall.* *p*

F Fmaj7 F7 D A7 A7-5

Tho' the days are long, Twi - light sings a
In the drear - y gray, Of an - oth - er

mp a tempo

D7 G7 Dm6 B♭m6 C6

song, Of the hap - pi - ness that used to
day, You'll be far a - way and I'll be

F
Dm
Am
D°7/A
be;
Soon my eyes will close,
blue;
Still I hope and pray,
Am
A°7
B°/A
C
E♭°7
G7
C♯°7
Soon I'll find re - pose,
And in dreams you're
Thru each wea - ry day,
For it brings the
Dm7
F/G
G7-9
C7
B♭/C
Chorus:
C
al - ways near to me.
I'll
night and dreams of you.
rall.
mp
Slowly (with expression)
B♭
B♭m6
See You In My Dreams.

F
F/A
G♯°7
E
D/A
F6
Hold you in my dreams,
D7/A
Am
D7
Some - one took you out of my arms,
G7
G6
G7
C6
C9
C6
C9
B♭m6/C
C7
Still I feel the thrill of your charms,
B♭
B♭m6
Lips that once were mine,

F
F/A
G♯°7
E
D/F
F6
Ten - der eyes that shine,
Am7-5
D7
Am7-5
D7
A/C♯
A7
Dm
C
They will light my way to - night, I'll
mf
B♭
B♭/D
B♭m6/D♭
4fr.
C7
1. F
A♭°7
See You In My Dreams.
dim.
mf
Gm7
3fr.
C7
2. F
D♭7
F6
I'll Dreams.
mp
rall.
p

Vera Zorina and George Raft

I'LL WALK ALONE

In 1944, Universal Studios came up with Follow The Boys, *a star-studded film to honor all the artists who entertained American troops during the war. This musical extravaganza featured Dinah Shore's performance of this great song, which was nominated for an Oscar that same year. Dinah's recording reached the top of the charts that same year.*

Words by SAMMY CAHN
Music by JULE STYNE

Moderato

f

N.C. G E7(♭9)

I'll Walk A - lone because to tell you the truth, I'll be

p mp

Am7 D7 Dm E7 A7

lone - ly. I don't mind be - ing lone - ly

mf

D7 Cm D7 G G+ Em A7 A♭7+ D9

When my heart tells me you are lone - ly too. I'll Walk A-

p

G
E7(♭9)
Am7
lone, they'll ask me why and I'll tell them I'd rath - er;
mp
D7 Dm E7 A7 D7 Cm D7
There are dreams I must gath - er, Dreams we fash-ioned the night
mf
G G+ G Dm7 G9 C
you held me tight. I'll al - ways be near you, wher-
p
Cm G D7 G
ev - er you are, Each night in ev - 'ry prayer. If
mf

Em6
F♯7
Em6
F♯7
Bm
Bm7
Bdim
you call I'll hear_ you, no mat - ter how far;_ Just close your eyes_ and I'll be
D9
D7(♭9)
D7
G
E7(♭9)
there._ Please walk a - lone_ and send your love and your kiss - es to
p
mp
Am7
D7
Dm
E7
A6
D7
G♯dim
Am7
D7(♭9)
guide me._ Till you're walk - ing be - side_ me,_ I'll Walk A -
mf
rit.
1.G
Em
A7
A7+
D9
a tempo
2.G
C6
G6
lone._ I'll Walk A - lone._
f

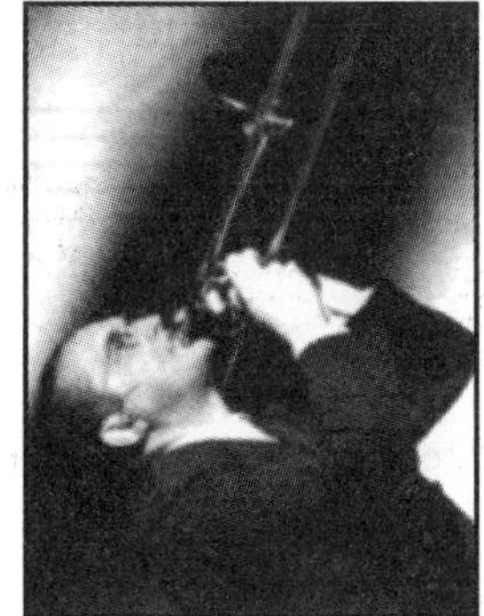

Tommy Dorsey

I'M GETTIN' SENTIMENTAL OVER YOU

Following the break-up of the Dorsey Brothers band, brother Tommy formed his own band; in 1936 be recorded his theme song and went on to earn his title, "The Sentimental Gentleman of Swing." The Ink Spots recorded this dreamy ballad in 1940 on the Decca label, and vocalist Jack Leonard followed up with his recording in 1941. The song was used on the soundtrack of 3 films, Keep 'Em Flying *(1941),* DuBarry Was A Lady *(1943), and* A Song Is Born *(1948).*

Very slow

Words by GEORGE BASSMAN
Music by NED WASHINGTON

mf

Eb7 D7sus D7

Verse

mp

I was just an - oth - er who

Db7 C+7 C7 F7 Bb7 Ebmaj7

laughed at ro - mance,—

I said it was not for me.—

Eb6 Bb+7 Eb7 D7sus D7

Then you made your en - trance and

D♭7
C+7
C7
F7
F9
B♭7
B♭dim7
Gm/B♭
B♭9
right at a glance
I knew this was meant to be.
Chorus
E♭maj7
D7sus
D7
B♭m/D♭
C+
C7
Nev - er thought I'd fall, but now I hear love call. I'm
p-mf
F9
B♭7
E♭6
(C7♭9/E
Fm6)
B♭9
Get - tin' Sen - ti - ment - al O - ver You.
E♭maj7
D7sus
D7
B♭m/D♭
C+
C7
Things you say and do just thrill me through and through, I'm
F9
B♭+7
B♭7
E♭
A♭6
E♭
D7
Gm
Cm/G
Get - ting Sen - ti - ment-al O - ver You.
I thought I was hap - py; I could

A7
Am7♭5
D7
D+
D7
live with - out love;
Now I must ad - mit love is
Gm
Gdim7
B♭7
E♭maj7
D7sus
D7
all I'm think - ing of.
Won't you please be kind and
B♭m/D♭
C+
C7
F9
B♭7
B♭+
just make up your mind that
you'll be sweet and gen - tle, be
E♭
B♭7/D
B♭m6/D♭
C+7
C7
F9
B♭+7
B♭7
gen - tle with me?
Be - cause I'm Sen - ti - ment - al O - ver
1. E♭
E♭dim7
B♭7
2. E♭
E♭6
You.
You.
sfz

I'M OLD-FASHIONED

In the 1942 film, You Were Never Lovelier, *Fred Astaire dances his way into Rita Hayworth's heart. This song gave her the opportunity (in the midst of all that tapping and whirling) to tell him a little bit about herself. Cast also included Adolphe Menjou and Xavier Cugat and his orchestra.*

This arrangement is playable on both piano or organ. Pianists should ignore the small organ pedal notes indicated in the bass clef.

General Electronic/Pipe Organs		Drawbar Organs	
Upper:	Flutes, String 8', (no 16')	Upper:	00 8833 322
Lower:	Horn 8', Cello 8'	Lower:	(00) 7676 512
Pedal:	Flute 16', 8'	Pedal:	46
Vibrato:	On/Normal	Animation:	Leslie On. Upper/Lower
		Organ:	Brilliance. Reverb. 1

Words by
JOHNNY MERCER

Music by
JEROME KERN
Arranged by
MARK LAUB

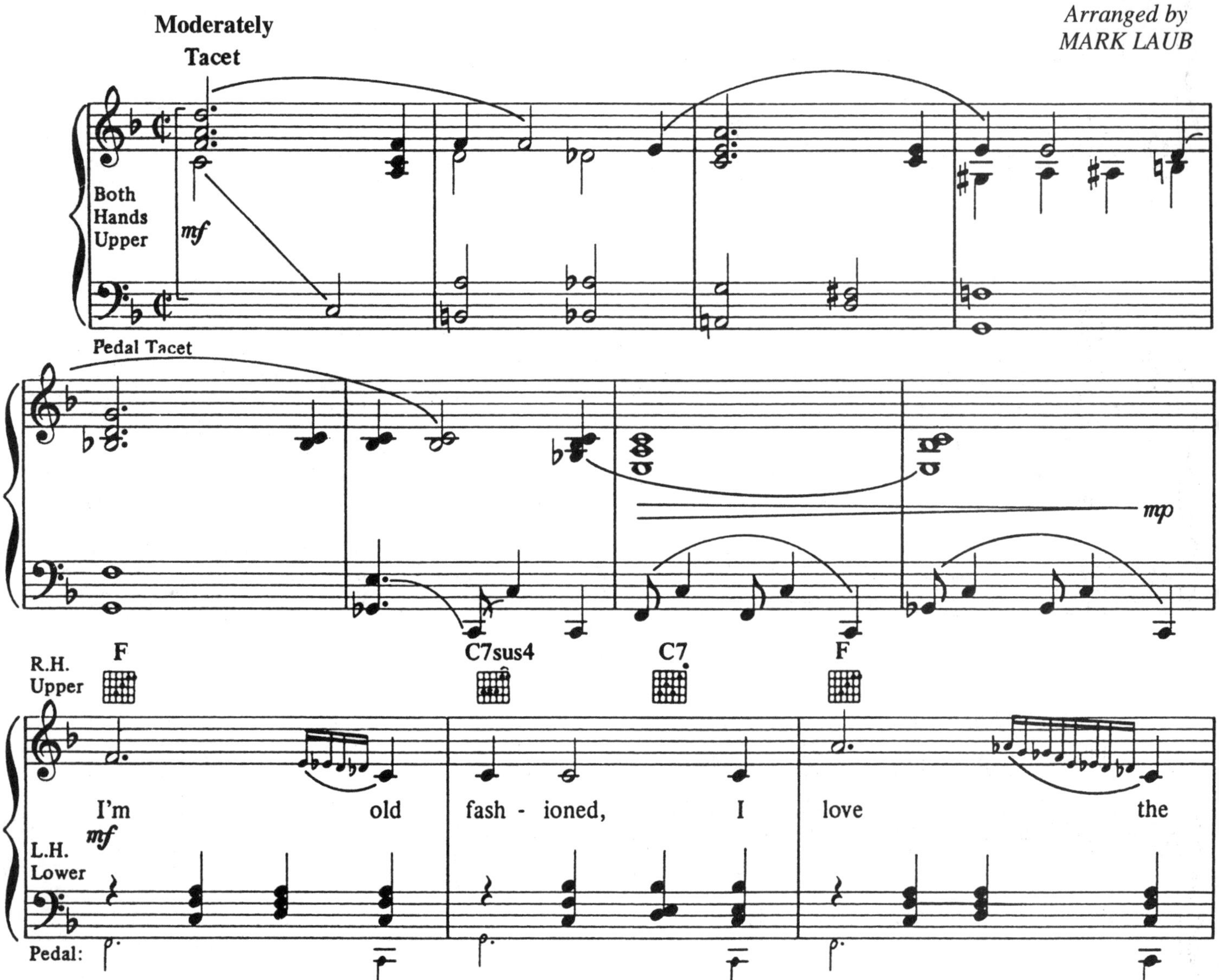

Moderately
Tacet
Both Hands Upper
mf
Pedal Tacet
mp
R.H. Upper
F C7sus4 C7 F
I'm old fashioned, I love the
mf
L.H. Lower
Pedal:

Am
C7
Fsus4
F
Am7
F6
moon - light, I
love the
old fash - ioned
Gm6
A7
Dm7
3
things
The
sound of
G7
Dm7
D9
D7
rain up -
on a win - dow
pane, The
Gm7
F♯7dim
Gm7
Am7
Gm7
G9/B
C7sus4
Cdim
C7
star - ry song that
A - pril
sings.
cresc. mp

Gm7
Cdim
C7
C+
F6
Gm7
C7♭9
This year's fan - cies are
Fmaj7
E7sus4
E7
A
E7
pass - ing fan - cies, But sigh - ing sighs,
Upper
mf
cresc.
A
D7
E7
Adim
Gm7
C9addA
hold - ing hands
These my heart un - der - stands.
f
R.H. Upper
F
C7sus4
C7
F
I'm old fash - ioned But I don't
L.H. Lower

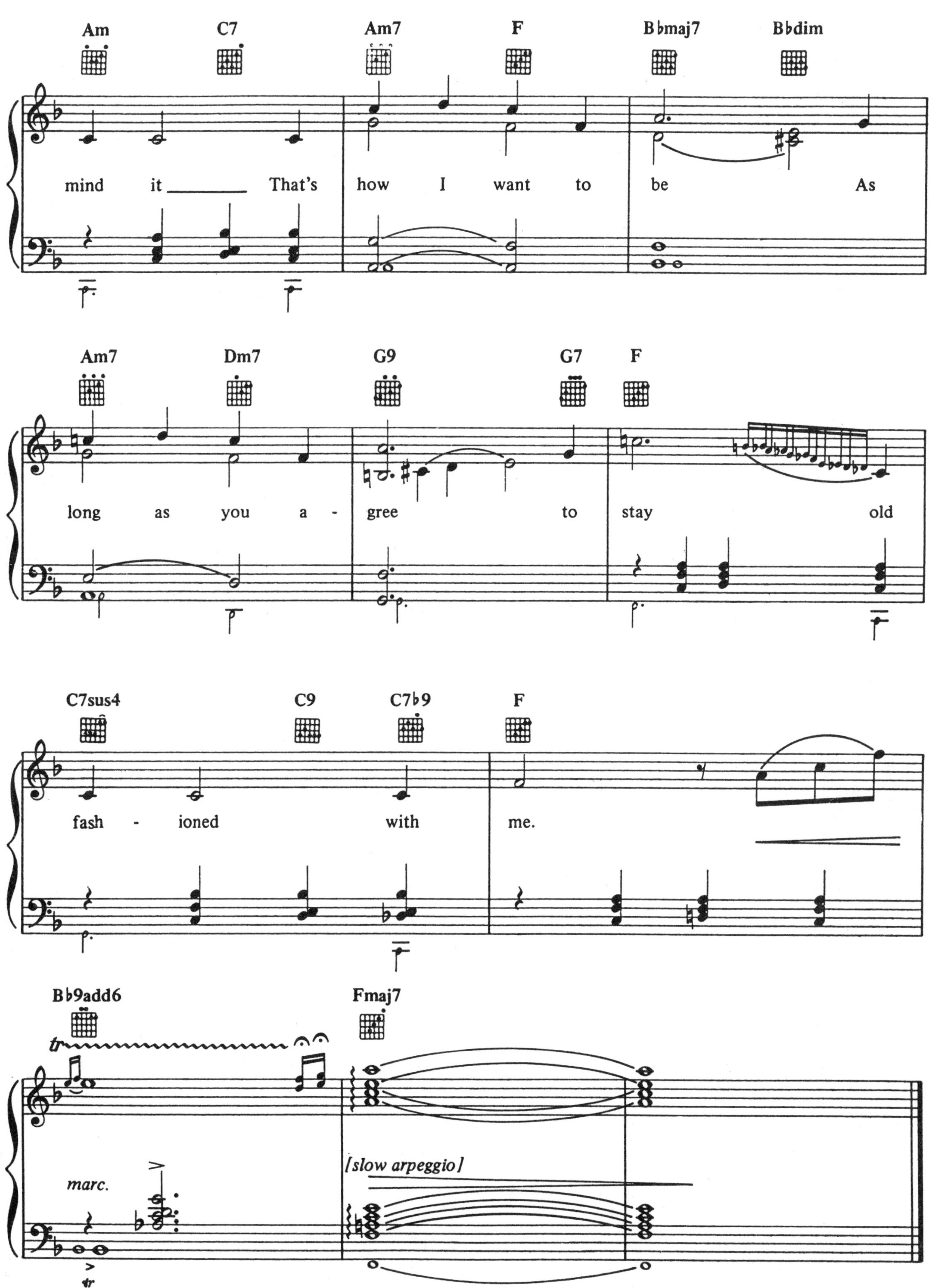
Am C7 Am7 F B♭maj7 B♭dim
mind it ___ That's how I want to be As
Am7 Dm7 G9 G7 F
long as you a - gree to stay old
C7sus4 C9 C7♭9 F
fash - ioned with me.
B♭9add6 Fmaj7
tr
marc.
[slow arpeggio]

Marilyn Monroe

I'M THRU WITH LOVE

Another many-movie song from Kahn. The films this time include such diverse titles as Honeymoon Lodge, The Affairs Of Dobie Gillis, *and* Some Like It Hot, *with a memorable Marilyn Monroe rendition. It's the classic romantic cliff-hanger, the hero's done with romance—sure, we believe it, but let's just sit tight for that last reel anyway!*

Words by
GUS KAHN
Music by
MATT MALNECK and
JOSEPH A. LIVINGSTON

Moderato

mf f

F Gm7 C7 F C7aug F

mf I have giv - en you my true love, but you love a new love,

Em7-5 C6 F C7aug F

What am I sup - posed to do now, with you now, you're thru now.

Am
E7
Cm6
D7
Gm
D7
B♭m6
C7
You'll be on your mer - ry way,
poco rit.
And there's on - ly this to say,
Chorus
Fmaj7/A
A♭dim
Gm
C7
Fmaj7
Faug
p
a tempo
I'm Thru with Love, I'll nev - er fall a - gain, Said "A - dieu" to love, "Don't
B♭
B♭m
F
Cm/A
D7
Gm
ev - er call a - gain" For I must have you or no one,
C7
C6
F
C7
Fmaj7/A
A♭dim
And so I'm Thru With Love. I've locked my heart, I'll

Gm
C7
Fmaj7
Faug
B♭
B♭m
keep my feel - ings there I have stocked my heart with i - cy frig - i - daire, And I
F
Cm/A
D7
Gm
C7
C6
mean to care for no one, Be - cause I'm Thru With
F
Am
F
Am6
F
Love.
mf
Why did you lead me to think you could care,
Am
F
D7
C
Caug
You did - n't need me, for you had your share, Of slaves a - round you to

Am
G7
C
Gm7
C6
C7
hound you and swear, with Deep e - mo - tion, de - vo - tion to you; Good -
Fmaj7/A
A♭dim
Gm
C7
Fmaj7
Faug
bye to Spring, and all it meant to me, It can nev - er bring the
B♭
B♭m
F
Cm/A
D7
Gm
thing that used to be, For I must have you or no one,
C7
C6
1.
F
C7
2.
F
B♭7
F
And so I'm Thru With Love. I'm Love.

Linda Ronstadt

I'VE GOT A CRUSH ON YOU

Presented as an upbeat number in the 1928 musical Treasure Girl *and the 1930 political satire* Strike Up The Band, *"I've Got A Crush On You" didn't become a lush, romantic ballad until Frank Sinatra recorded it in 1948. The Sinatra-type rendition was featured in the films* Meet Danny Wilson *and* Three For The Show. *Linda Ronstadt carried the Ol' Blue Eyes' tradition into the new era with her 1983 version (available on the platinum album* What's New, *Asylum 60260).*

Music and Lyrics by
GEORGE GERSHWIN and IRA GERSHWIN

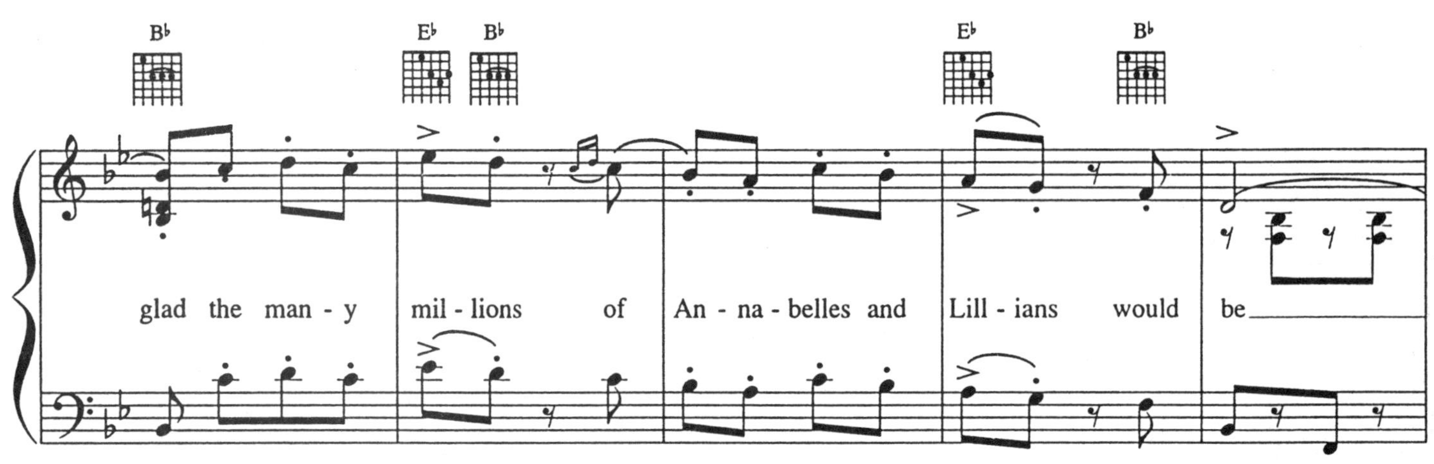

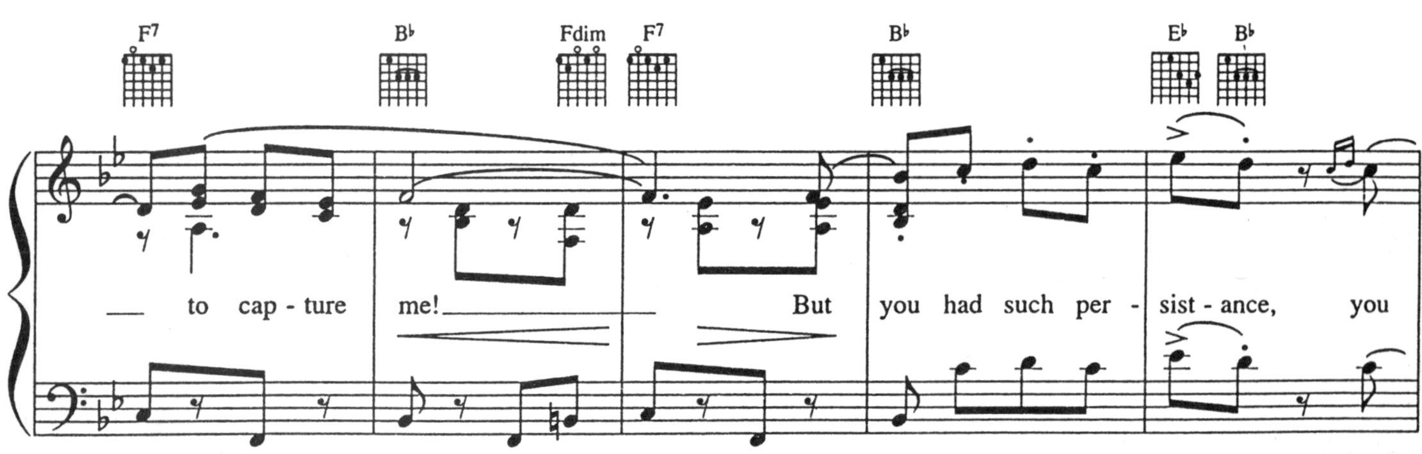

E♭
B♭
D
A7
D
wore down my re - sist - ance: I fell, and it was swell.
Cm7
F7
B♭
B♭dim
Cm7
F7
B♭6
Cm7
F7
Ann: You're my big and brave and hand - some Ro - me - o. How I
B♭
B♭maj7
B♭6
C7
F7
B♭
E♭
B♭
won you I shall nev - er, nev - er know, Timothy: It's not that you're at - trac - tive, but,
E♭
Gm7
C7
F7
E♭m6
F7
oh my heart grew ac - tive, when you came in - to view.

Refrain
B♭maj7
A9
E♭
Cm7
F7
p – mf
I've got a crush on you, sweetie pie,
B♭maj7
A7
All the day and night-time hear me sigh. I
B♭
Gm7
C7
B7
never had the least notion that I could
C9
B9
F7
C+
Bbmaj7
fall with so much emotion. Could you coo?
p

Cm7 F7 B♭maj7 A7
Could you care for a cun - ning cot - tage
Cm7 D7+5 D7 Gm7 Am Gm7 C9
we could share? The world will par - don my
F6 B♭maj7 B♭6 C9 A6 F7
mush, 'cause I've got a crush my ba - by, on
fz
mf
1. B♭ Gm6 Cm7 F7
you. I've got a
mf
2. B♭ Gm6 F7 B♭
you.
fz

Marion Hutton, Glenn Miller and Tex Beneke

I'VE GOT A GAL IN KALAMAZOO

Legend has it that Warren originally devised this piece as a rhythmic exercise, and that it took the insight of lyricist Mack Gordon to realize it could make the perfect follow up to the duo's "Chattanooga Choo-Choo." True or not, the tune's catchy syncopation bounced it all the way to the top of the charts in an all-star recording featuring Glenn Miller and his Orchestra, Marion Hutton, Tex Benecke, The Modernaires, and The Nicholas Brothers.

Words by MACK GORDON
Music by HARRY WARREN

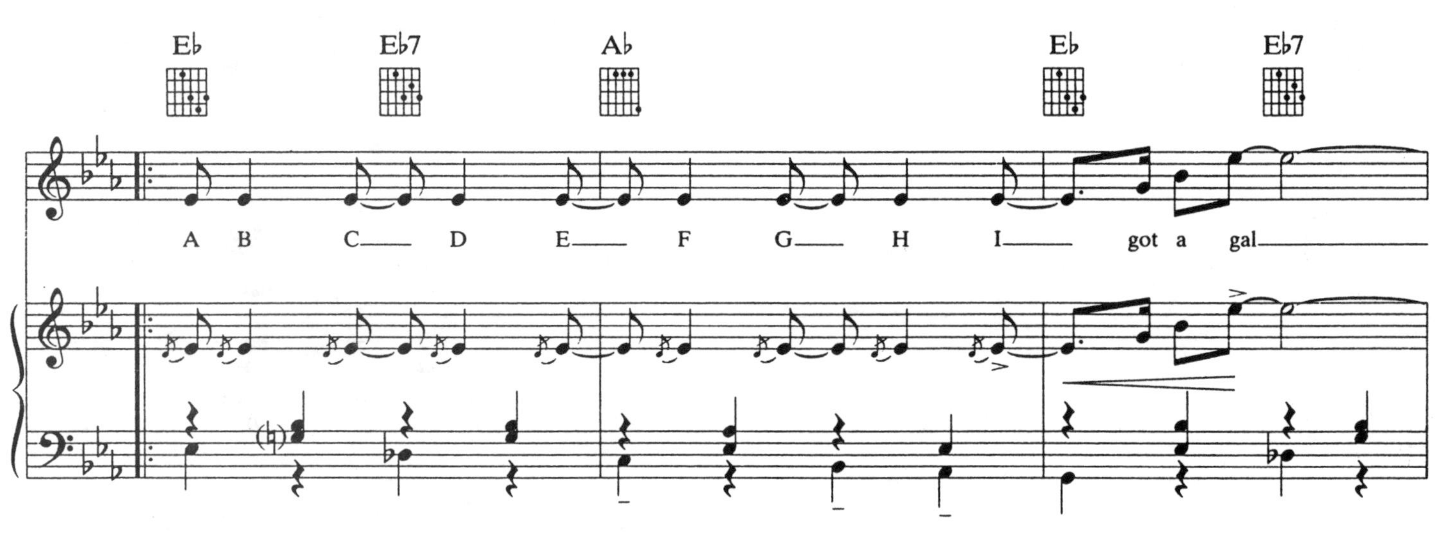

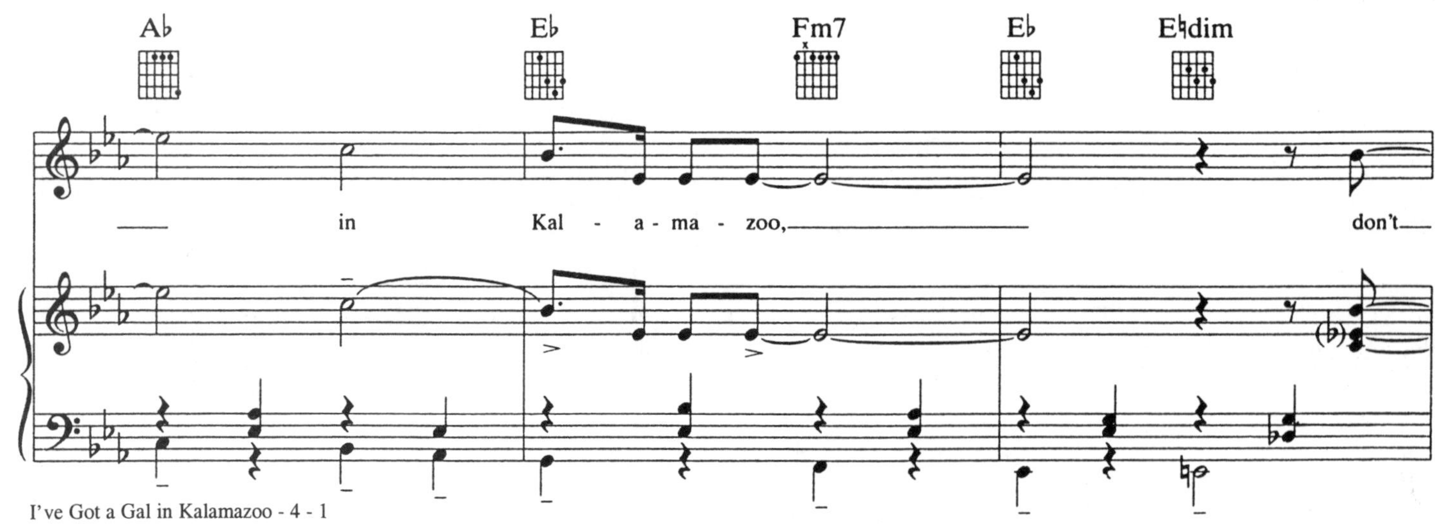

Fm7 B♭7 Fm7 B♭7 E♭ E♭7
— wan - na boast, — but I know — she's the toast — of Kal - a - ma - zoo — zoo zoo —
A♭ E♭ E♭7 A♭
— zoo zoo — zoo. Years — have gone by, — my,
E♭ Fm7 E♭ E♮dim Fm7 B♭7
my, how she grew, — I — liked her looks, — when I car -
Fm7 B♭7 E♭ E♭7 A♭ E♭
ried her books — in Kal - a - ma - zoo — zoo zoo — zoo zoo. — I'm gon - na

G7+5
G7♭9
G7+5
G7♭9
C7♭9
B♭m6
send a wire, hop - pin' on a fly - er leav - in' to - day.
C7
F 7♭9
Am I dream - in' I can hear her scream - in' "Hy -
B♭/A♭
B♭dim/G
Fm7
Cm6
C♭7+5
B♭7
E♭
E♭7
a Mis - ter Jack - son" ev - 'ry - thing's O K - A - L - A - M -
A♭
E♭
E♭7
A♭
A - Z - O Oh, what a gal, a

E♭ Fm7 E♭ E♮dim Fm7 B♭7
real pip - per - oo; I'll make my bid for that freck -
Fm7 B♭7 G7+5 C7 F7 B♭9
le faced kid, I'm hur - ry - ing to, I'm goin' to Mich - i - gan to
E♭ E♭7 A♭ A♭m B♭7 E♭ E♭7 A♭ B♭7 A♭
see the sweet - est gal in Kal - a - ma - zoo.
2.
E♭ E♭7 A♭ E♭ A°7 B♭7 E♭
zoo zoo zoo zoo zoo! Kal - a - ma - zoo!

I'VE GROWN ACCUSTOMED TO HER FACE

Lyrics by
ALAN JAY LERNER

Introduced by the incomparable Rex Harrison as Henry Higgins in My Fair Lady *in 1956. One of the greatest Broadway musicals of all time which also starred Julie Andrews as Liza Doolittle, the show ran for 2,717 performances.*

Music by
FREDERICK LOEWE

Eb Ebmaj7 Eb6 Fm7 Bb7
na - ture to me now; Like breath - ing out and breath-ing in
na - ture to me now; Like breath - ing out and breath-ing in
Ebmaj7 Eb6 Ab6 D7 Eb C7+5
I was se - rene - ly in - de - pen - dent and con - tent be - fore we met;
I'm ver - y grate - ful she's a wo - man and so eas - y to for - get;
Fm7 Bb7 G+ C7+5 F9 Abm
Sure - ly I could al - ways be that way a - gain and yet, I've grown ac - cus - tomed to her looks; Ac -
Rath - er like a ha - bit one can al - ways break and yet, I've grown ac - cus - tomed to the trace of
Eb Gm7 Fm7 Bb9 Eb Eb
cus - tomed to her voice; Ac - cus - tomed to her face. I've Grown Ac - Face.
some - thing in the air; Ac - cus - tomed to her face. I've Grown Ac - Face.

Paula Kelly, Shirley MacLaine and Chita Rivera

IF MY FRIENDS COULD SEE ME NOW!

Shirley MacLaine performed this great hit from Sweet Charity *in the film version as the warm-hearted but unlucky dance hostess. Sammy Davis, Linda Clifford and composer Cy Coleman had discs, among many others.*

Music by
CY COLEMAN
Words by
DOROTHY FIELDS

Strut tempo

C

To - night at eight you should - a seen

G7

a chauf - feur pull up in a rent - ed lim - ou - sine!

Ab7 G7

My neigh-bors burned! They like to die! When I

Ab7 G7

tell them who is get - tin' in and go - in' out is I! 1. If they could

f

C
C7
(1.) see me now, that lit - tle gang of mine, I'm
(2.) see me now, my lit - tle dust - y group,
(3.) see me now, a - lone with Mis - ter V., Who's
F
eat - ing fan - cy chow and drink - ing fan - cy wine. I'd like those
Traip - sin' 'round this mil - lion dol - lar chick - en coop. I'd hear those
wait - in' on me like he was a mai - tre d'. I hear my
B7
E7
Am
stum - ble bums to see for a fact The kind of
thrift shop cats say: "Broth - er, get her! Draped on a
bud - dies say - ing: "Cra - zy, what gives? To - night she's
D7
Fm6
C
D7
G7
top - drawer, first - rate chums I at - tract. All I can
bed - spread made from three kinds of fur." All I can
liv - ing like the oth - er half lives." To think the

C
C7
say is, "Wow - ee! Look - a where I am. To - night I
say is, "Wow! Wait till the riff and raff See just ex -
high - est brow, which I must say is he, Should pick the
F
E7
land - ed, pow! right in a pot of jam." What a
act - ly how he signed this au - to - graph." What a
low - est brow, which there's no doubt is me. What a
A7+5
Bb9
G7
A7
D7
Tacet
set up! Ho - ly cow!
build - up! Ho - ly cow!
step up! Ho - ly cow!
They'd nev-er be - lieve it, If My
G7
G#dim
F
G7
C
G7
1. 2.
3.
Friends Could See Me Now!
2. If they could
3. If they could

The Kingston Trio

IT WAS A VERY GOOD YEAR

Good songs never go out of style—a point proven by this song, which was introduced in 1961 by the Kingston Trio. It's now enjoying newfound popularity, thanks to the inclusion of Frank Sinatra's 1966 version in Spike Lee's latest hit film, Jungle Fever.

Words and Music by
ERVIN DRAKE

Moderately

mf *rit.* *a tempo* *mf*

Dm Eb Dm

1. When I was sev - en - teen, It was a ver - y good year, It was a ver - y good year for
(2. When I was) twen - ty - one, It was a ver - y good year, It was a ver - y good year for
(3. When I was) thir - ty - five, It was a ver - y good year, It was a ver - y good year for
(4. But now the) days are short, I'm in the au - tumn of the year; And now I think of my life as

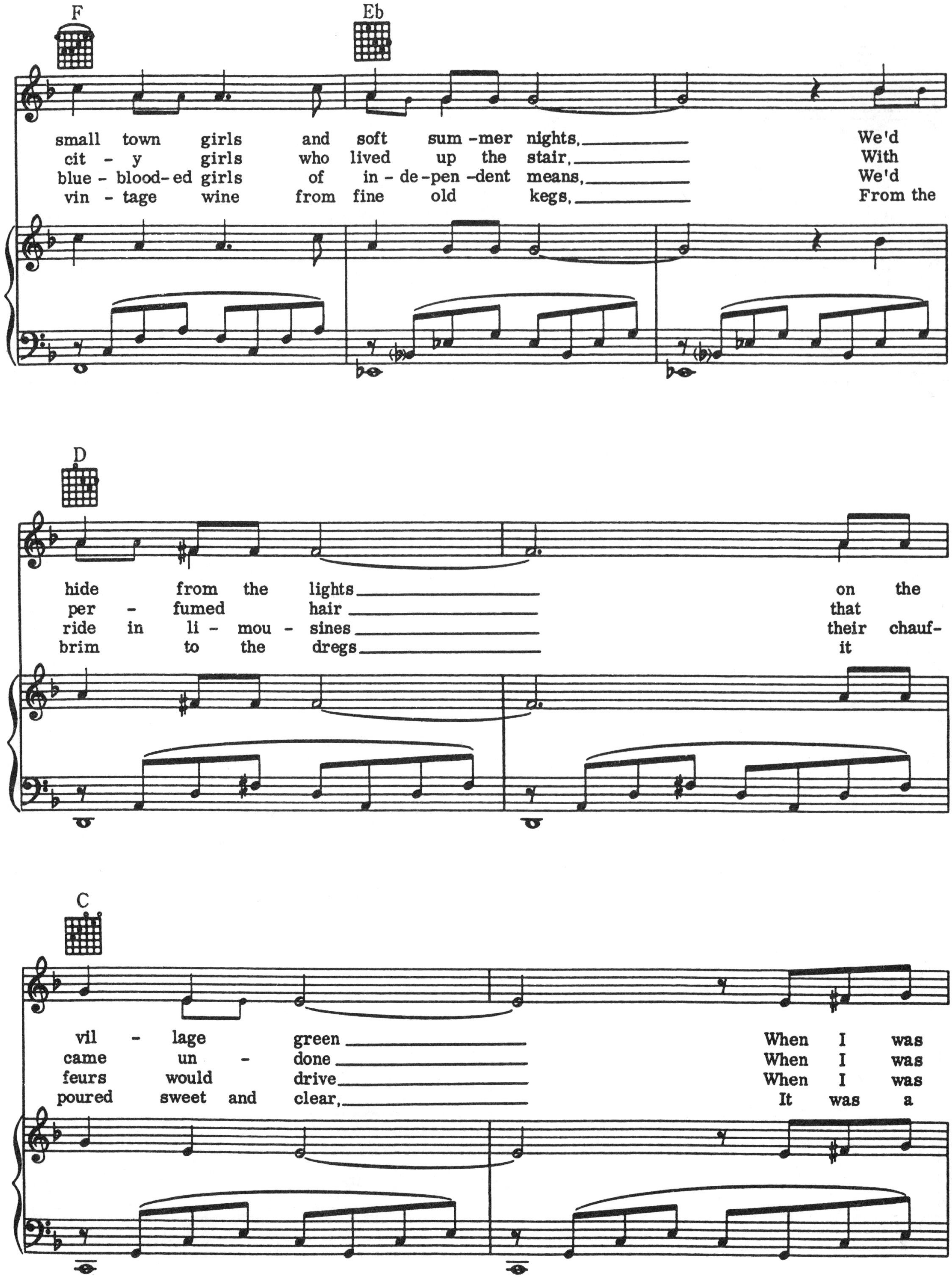

F Eb

small town girls and soft sum - mer nights, We'd
cit - y girls who lived up the stair, With
blue - blood - ed girls of in - de - pen - dent means, We'd
vin - tage wine from fine old kegs, From the

D

hide from the lights on the
per - fumed hair that
ride in li - mou - sines their chauf-
brim to the dregs it

D
sev - en - teen!
twen - ty - one!
thir - ty - five!
ver - y good year!
Dm
(Whistle first and last time)
Am
F
(last time poco a poco rit.)
1. 2. 3.
A7
4.
A7
A
2. When I was
3. When I was
4. But now the
poco rit.
pp

Betty Hutton in *Incendiary Blonde*

IT HAD TO BE YOU

Isham Jones introduced his wonderful song in 1924 and garnered a no. 1 disk. Over the years, Cliff Edwards, Billy Murray with Aileen Stanley, Paul Whiteman, Helen Forrest with Dick Haymes, Betty Hutton and Artie Shaw all had Top Ten recordings. A highlight of the films Incendiary Blonde, I'll See You In My Dreams, Show Business *and* South Sea Sinner, *"It Had To Be You" was most recently featured in the 1989 hit flick* When Harry Met Sally, *as performed by the talented newcomer Harry Connick, Jr. (available on the gold soundtrack album, Columbia 45319).*

Words by
GUS KAHN
Music by
ISHAM JONES

Moderate swing

G/B Bbdim7 Am7-5 D7+5 D13 G/B Eb7/Bb Am7 D7-9 D7

G Gmaj7 G7 C6 Cm6 G/B Em7

Why do I do just as you say? Why must I just give you your way?
Seems like dreams like I always had, could be, should be making me glad.

A7 D13 G Cm6/A D7+5 G D7/A Gdim7/Bb

Why do I sigh? Why don't I try to forget? It must have
Why am I blue? It's up to you to explain. I'm thinking

G
Gmaj7
G7
C6
Cm6
G/B
Em7
been that some - thing lov - ers call fate; kept on say - ing I had to wait.
may - be, ba - by, I'll go a - way. Some day, some way you'll come and say,
A7
D9 4fr
E♭9-5 5fr
D9 4fr
D+
I saw them all; just could - n't fall 'till we met.
"It's you I need," and you'll be plead - ing in vain.
It had to be you.
G
D+
G
E7
It had to be you.
A7
I wan - dered a - round and fin - al - ly found the some - bod - y who

D7
could make me be true,
D♯dim7
Em
A7
could make me be blue
and e - ven be glad,
just to be sad,
D9
E♭9-5
5fr.
D9
4fr.
D+
G
D+
think - ing of you.
Some oth - ers I've seen
G
E7
might nev - er be mean,
might nev - er be cross,

A7
or try to be boss,
but they would - n't do.
Em
Am
Am7
Adim7
D7
G
B7/F♯
For no - bod - y else
gave me a thrill.
With all your faults,
I love you still.
Em
Gdim7/B♭
D7
Gdim7/B♭
D7
It had to be you,
won - der - ful you,
had to be you.
1.
G
Gdim7/B♭
Cm6/A
D7
D+
It had to be you.
2.
G
Cm6
G6

THE LAST TIME I SAW PARIS

This Song was written a week after the Germans took over the French capital during World War II. Hammerstein was so depressed by the fall of the city that he couldn't keep his mind on the show he was doing and wrote the lyrics on the spur of the moment to relieve his mental anguish. The lyrics were then sent to Kern who composed the music. This was a complete departure from their usual method of collaboration—Kern usually writing the music before Hammerstein wrote the words. It captured the Oscar in 1941, when it appeared in the film, Lady Be Good, *performed by Ann Sothern.*

This arrangement is playable on both piano or organ. Pianists should ignore the small organ pedal notes indicated in the bass clef.

Arranged for Piano or Organ by MARK LAUB

General Electronic/Pipe Organs
Upper: Tibia 8', 2', Quint. Flute 2 2/3
Lower: Flute 8', 4', Dulciana 8'
Pedal: Bourdon 16', Flute 8'
Vibrato: On/Normal

Drawbar Organs
Upper: 00 8008 001
Lower: (00) 0777 00(0)
Pedal: 55
Animation: Leslie on. Upper/Lower
Organ: Brilliance. Reverb. 1

Words by OSCAR HAMMERSTEIN II
Music by JEROME KERN

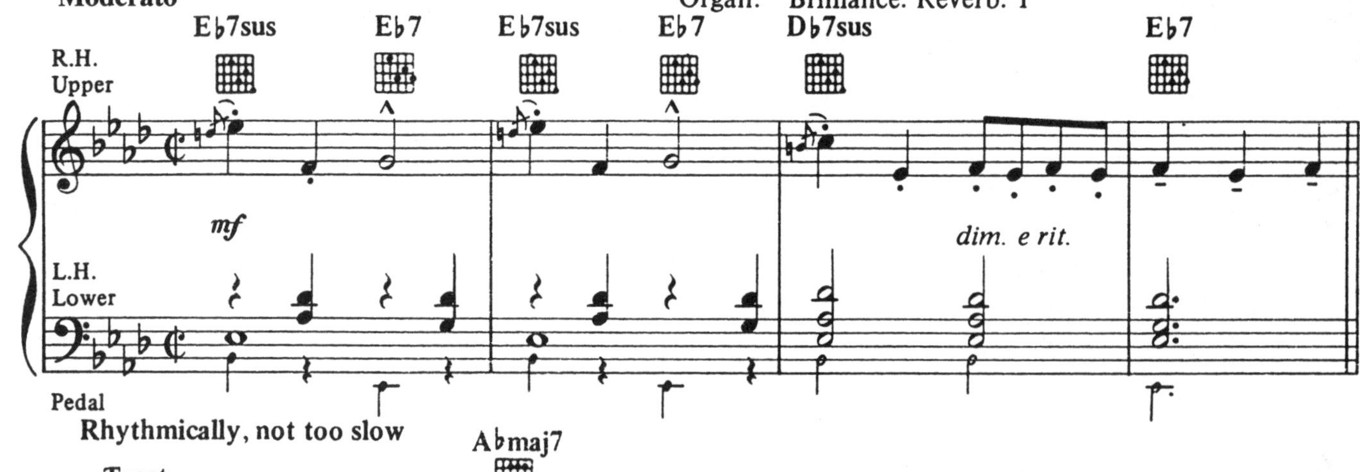

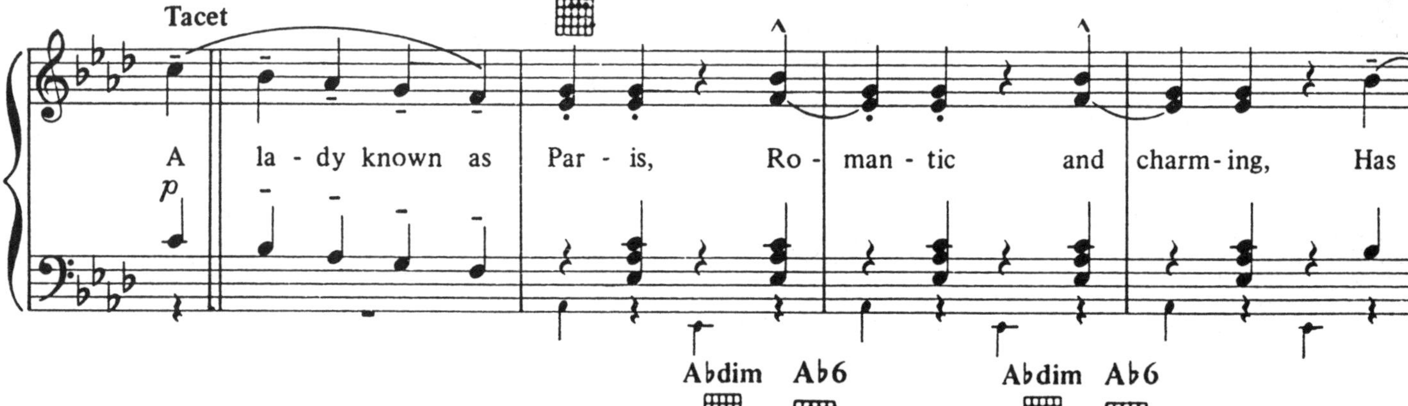

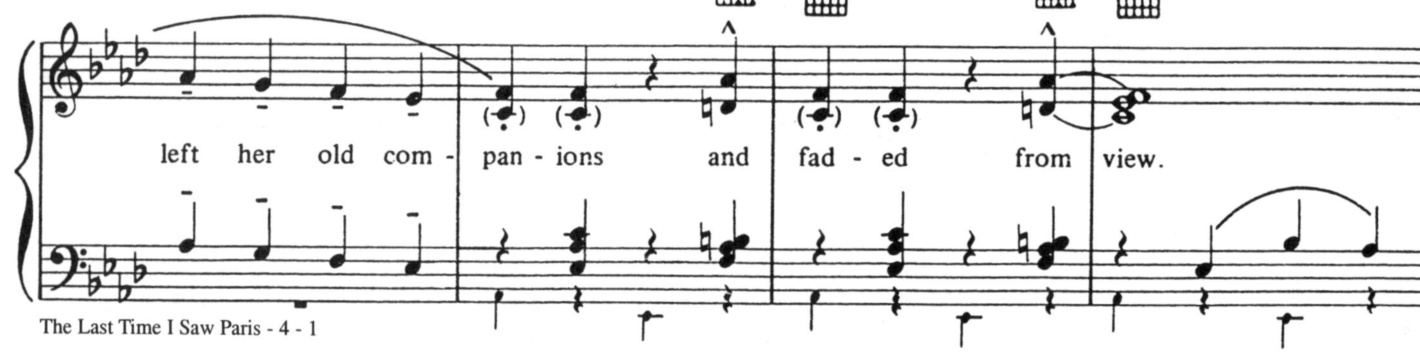

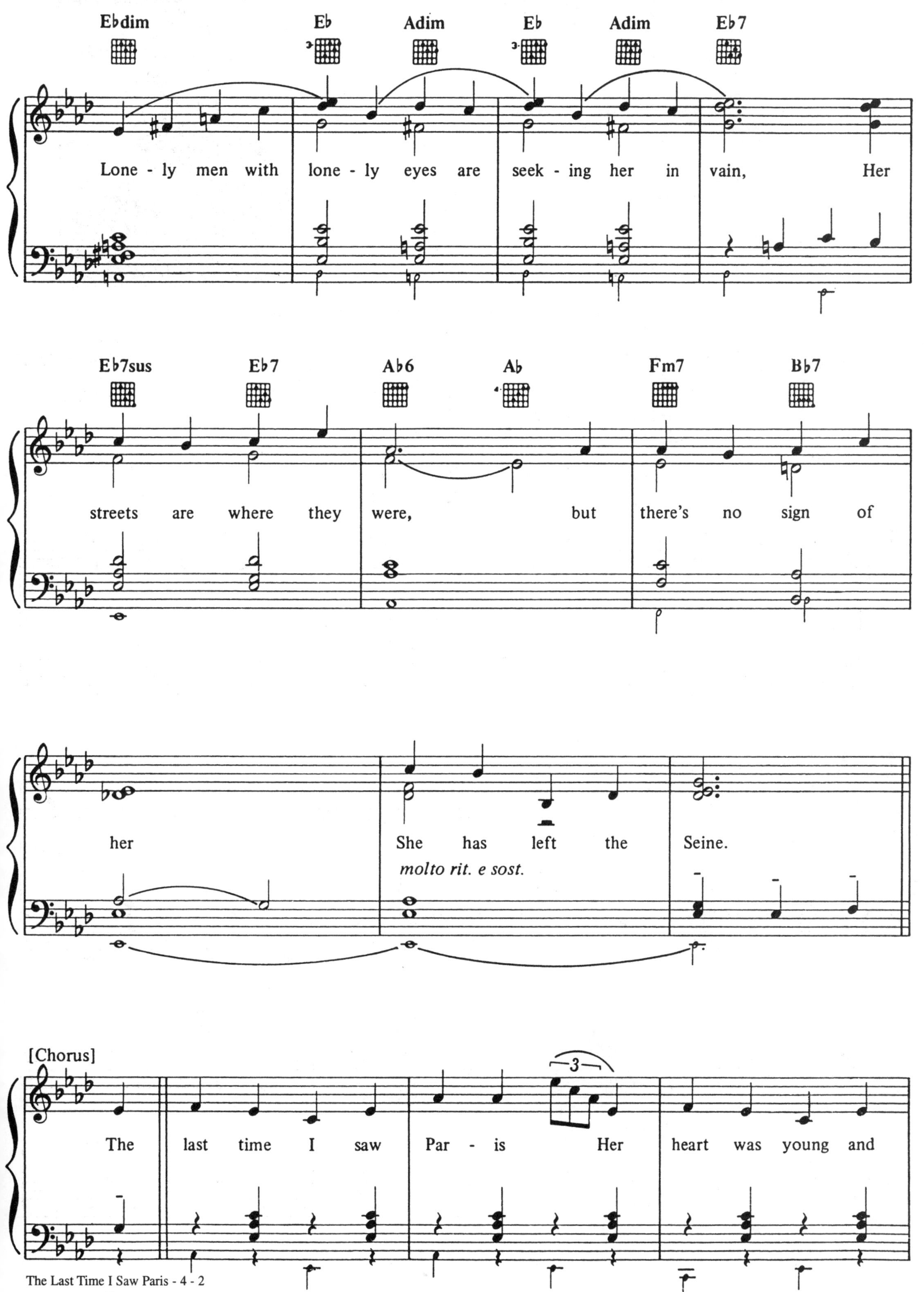

E♭dim
E♭
Adim
E♭
Adim
E♭7
Lone - ly men with lone - ly eyes are seek - ing her in vain, Her
E♭7sus
E♭7
A♭6
A♭
Fm7
B♭7
streets are where they were, but there's no sign of
her She has left the Seine.
molto rit. e sost.
[Chorus]
The last time I saw Par - is Her heart was young and
3

Eb7
Dbm6
Eb7
Bbm7
Eb7
gay, I heard the laugh - ter of her heart in ev - 'ry street ca -
Ab
fé. The last time I saw Par - is, Her trees were dressed for
mf
Eb7
Dbm6
Eb7
Bbm7
Eb7
spring, And lov - ers walked be - neath those trees and birds found songs to
Ab
[Brightly]
Bb7
Eb
Bb7
sing. I dodged the same old tax - i - cabs that I had dodged for
Upper
Pedal Tacet

E♭
C7
F
B♭m7
R.H. Upper
years; The cho - rus of their squeak - y horns was mu - sic to my
L.H. Lower
Pedal:
E♭7sus
E♭7
A♭
3
ears The last time I saw Par - is Her heart was young and
mp
E♭7
B♭m7
E♭7
E♭m6
F7
B♭m7
E♭7♭9
3
gay. No mat - ter how they change her I'll re - mem-ber her that
mf
ritardando
dim.
A♭
A♭maj7+6
A♭maj7+6
A♭maj7+6
A♭maj9+6
way.
a tempo
ritard.

Dana Andrews in *Laura*

LAURA

Of all the wonderful music that has flowed from David Raksin, his theme for the film Laura *is certainly the most acclaimed. The piece has become a true standard and has been recorded numerous times, both with and without Johnny Mercer's haunting lyrics, added after the film's release. Among the 400-plus recordings are those by Woody Herman, Freddy Martin, Stan Kenton, Frank Sinatra and Raksin's own RCA/BMG CD, with the Philharmonia Symphony of London. The composer himself has honored us with the new arrangement below, which we are delighted to share with you.*

Lyric by
JOHNNY MERCE
Music by
DAVID RAKSIN

Andante

poco rall.

Verse

Gadd9 G Am7/G D7/G Gmaj7 Am7 D9

5 You know the feel - ing of some - thing half re - mem - bered of

a tempo

Gadd9 G G♯dim E7 Am7 D9 B♭ B♭m(♯11)

9 some - thing that nev - er hap - pened. Yet you re - call it well. You know the

Cm7
C♭9
B♭add9
Gm7
Em7-5
A7+
A6/9
A7+
14
poco ten.
feel - ing of rec - og - niz - ing some - one that you've nev - er met, as far as you could
poco ten.
Chorus
Moderato
Am7/D
B♭m7/E♭
E♭7
Am9
D7♭9♯5
Gmaj9
G6
fr5
fr5
fr3
19
tell; well: Lau - ra is the face in the mis - ty light,
poco dim.
mp
mf
Gm9
C7♭9♯5
Fmaj9
F6/9
24
foot - steps. that you hear down the hall,

Fm7
B♭7sus
B♭7
E♭maj7
E♭6
Am7-5
D7-9-5
29
The laugh that floats on a sum - mer night That you can nev - er quite
D9-5
D9
Bm7
E7♭9♯5
Am9
D7♭9♯5
34
poco rall.
a tempo
re - call, And you see Lau - ra on the train that is
G°(add maj7 9)
Gmaj13
Gm9
C7♭9♯5
39
pass - ing through, Those eyes how fa - mil - iar they

Fdim(add maj 7 9)
F6/9
Fm7
Fm6
C6/9
43
seem.
She gave your ve - ry first kiss to you,
D9
D7-9
Dm7
Dm7/G
1. Cadd9
A13-9
Dm9
E7-5
E7
48
that was Lau - ra but she's on - ly a dream.
2. Cadd9
A13-9
Dm9
E7-5
E7+5
Am(9)
Fm(♭6)
Fm6
G9sus
Cadd9
53
dream.
rit.

Sammy Fain

LOVE IS A MANY-SPLENDORED THING

From the 1955 film of the same title, starring Jennifer Jones and William Holden, this song was a hit by the Four Aces (Al Alberts, Dave Mahoney, Lou Silvestri and Sod Vocarro). It spent a couple weeks at no. 1 and became their fifth gold record. Other recordings by Don Cornell, David Rose and Woody Herman led this song to become a "Fifty-Year Hit Parade" selection.

Lyric by PAUL FRANCIS WEBSTER
Music by SAMMY FAIN

Moderately *(not too fast)*

mf

poco rit.

Freely

Eb Bb9

I walked a - long the streets of Hong Kong

mp

Eb Fm7 Bb7

town, up and down, up and

Eb Bb9

down. I met a lit - tle girl in Hong Kong

Eb
F7
Bb
town, And I said, "Can you tell me, please,
where's that love I've never found?
Fm7
Un-rav-el me this
Bb7
rid-dle. what is love? What can it be?" And
ten.
Bb9
Bbdim
in her eyes were but-ter-flies as she re-plied to me.
colla voce
poco rit.

Refrain, Moderately (not too fast)
Eb
Cm
Gm
Eb7
LOVE ___ IS A MAN-Y-SPLEN-DORED THING, ___ It's the
mp-mf
Ab
Ab6
Abmaj7
Fm6
Cm
Fm6
Cm
A-pril rose that on-ly grows in the ear-ly Spring; ___ Love is
Fm7
Cm7
Fm6
G7-9
na-ture's way of giv-ing a rea-son to be liv-ing, The
Cm
Cm7
D7
Am7
D7
G
Bb7
gold-en crown that makes a man a king. ___

Eb
Cm
Gm
Eb7
Once on a high and wind - y hill, In the
Ab
Abmaj7
Ab6
Ab
Gm7
C9
Gm7
C7
morn - ing mist two lov - ers kissed and the world stood still, Then your
Fm
Fm7
Fm6
G7+5
C7+5
C7
F7
Abm6
Eb
Cm
fin - gers touched my si - lent heart and taught it how to sing, Yes, true LOVE'S
poco rit.
slower
Fm7
Bb7-9
1. Eb
Fm7
Bb7-9
2. Eb
Fm7
Eb
A MAN - Y - SPLEN - DORED THING. THING.
allarg.
rall.

LOVER MAN
(Oh, Where Can You Be?)

What happens to a melody that lends itself to great instrumental renditions with lyrics that are made to order for female vocalists? It becomes one of the great jazz standards. "Lover Man" is such a song. Performed by instrumentalists Coleman Hawkins and Johnny Smith, and singers Dinah Washington, Diana Ross and Barbra Streisand, its most notable recording was Billie Holiday's 1944 Decca release.

Words and Music by
JIMMY DAVIS, ROGER "RAM" RAMIREZ
and JIMMY SHERMAN
Arranged by MARTY GOLD

Slowly

mf

Verse *(Freely)*

Am7 Gm7-5 C6 C♯dim Dm

I don't wish for rich - es,

G9 G9+ C9+ Am7 Gm7-5 C6 C♯dim

I'll not take the chance. Don't want to be

Dm A7-9 Gm9 Gm7 C11 C7-9 F A7 A7+

fa - mous, I on - ly want ro - mance.

Refrain:
(Blues tempo)
Dm7
G7
Dm7
G7
I don't know why, but I'm feel - ing so sad.
The night is cold, and I'm so all a - lone.
simile
C9
Gm7
C9
C7
I long to try some - thing I've nev - er had,
I'd give my soul just to call you my own,
F7+9
B♭9
Nev - er had no kiss - in' Oh, what I've been miss - in'.
Got a moon a - bove me, but no one to love me,
E♭7
B♭m
C9
Gm7/C
1.
F
Gm
F
A7+
Lov - er Man, oh where can you be?

2.
F
Gm
F
B♭maj7
Am7
Am7-5
be?
I've heard it said that the
D7
D9
D7-9
G6
Em6
E♭7
thrill of ro - mance can
be like a heav - en - ly
G6/D
Am7
D7
Gm7
Gm7-5
dream.
I go to bed with a
C7
C9
C7-9
F6
E♭7
prayer that you'll make love to
me, Strange as it

Em7-5
A7
Dm7
G7
seems.
Some day we'll meet and you'll
Dm7
G7
C9
Gm7
dry all my tears,
Then whis - per sweet lit - tle
C9
C7
F7
things in my ears,
Hug - gin' and a kiss - in',
B♭9
E♭7
B♭m
C9
Gm7/C
F
Gm
F
F13
Oh, what we've been miss - in',
Lov - er Man, oh where can you
be?
ff

Michelle Pfeiffer

MAKIN' WHOOPEE!

If you've ever doubted the staying power of an oldie but goodie, this tune will certainly change your mind! First performed by Eddie Cantor in Whoopee *in 1928, "Makin' Whoopee!" soon became his theme song. Such notables as Ray Charles, Count Basie and Paul Whitman have all recorded it, but it wasn't until 1989 that its popularity virtually exploded. The lovely Michelle Pfeiffer sang it in the smash summer flick,* The Fabulous Baker Boys *and blues singer/pianist Dr. John won a grammy for his duet rendition with pop star Rickie Lee Jones.*

Lyric by GUS KAHN
Music by WALTER DONALDSON

Moderato

Verse

G C7 G C7 G D B♭7 D B♭7 E7 A7

Ev-'ry-time I hear that march from Loh-en-grin I am al-ways on the out-side look-ing in May-be that is why I see the fun-ny side When I see a fall-en broth-er

Makin' Whoopie! - 4 - 1

D7
E7
take a bride.
Wed - dings make a lot of peo - ple
Am
A7
D7
sad, But if you're not the groom they're not so bad.
Chorus
G
D7
An - oth - er bride an - oth - er June An - oth - er
year or may - be less What's this I
p-f
G
G7
C
Am7
Am7-5
G
sun - - ny hon - ey - moon An - oth - er sea - son, an - oth - er
hear? well, can't you guess? She feels neg - lect - ed, and he's sus -

Eb7
D7
G
Cm/Eb
D7
G
rea - son for mak-in' whoop-ee! A lot of shoes a lot of
pect - ed of mak-in' whoop-ee! She sits a - lone 'most ev-'ry
D7
G
G7
C
Am7
Am7-5
rice the groom is nerv - ous he an-swers twice It's real-ly
night he does-n't 'phone her he does-n't write He says he's
G
Eb7
D7
G
kill - ing that he's so will - ing to make whoop-ee!
"bu - sy" but she says "is he?" he's makin' whoop-ee!
Ddim
Am
Cm6
G
Pic-ture a lit-tle love-nest, Down where the ros-es cling,
He does-n't make much mon-ey, On - ly five thou-sand per,

Ddim Am Cm6 G
Pic-ture the same sweet love-nest, Think what a year can bring. He's wash-ing
Some judge who thinks he's fun-ny, Says "you'll pay six to her." He says, "now
D7 G G7
dish-es and ba-by clothes He's so am-bit-ious he ev-en
judge, sup-pose I fail" The judge says "budge right in-to
C Am7 Am7-5 G Eb7 D7
sews But don't for-get, folks that's what you get, folks, for mak-in'
jail You'd bet-ter keep her, I think it's cheap-er, than mak-in'
1. G D7 2. G D G
whoop-ee! An-oth-er whoop-ee!

Johnny Mathis

MISTY

Introduced in 1954 as an instumental by the masterful Erroll Garner Trio, "Misty" later became a megahit, thanks to Johnny Mathis' 1959 recording (on the no. 1 gold album Heavenly, *Columbia 1351). Everlastingly popular, it served as the guiding vision for the 1971 film* Play Misty For Me. *Aside from Elvis Presley and Frank Sinatra, Billboard ranks Johnny as the top album artist from 1955 to 1985.*

Words by
JOHNNY BURKE
Music by
ERROLL GARNER

Slowly, with expression

mf

B♭9 E♭maj7 B♭m7 E♭7(♭9) A♭maj7

Refrain:

Look at me, I'm as help - less as a kit - ten up a tree, and I feel like I'm

A♭m D♭9 E♭maj7 Cm Fm7 B♭7(♭9) G7(♭5) C7

cling - ing to a cloud; I can't __ un - der - stand, __ I get mist - y just hold - ing your hand. __

F7(♭5) B♭7 B♭9 E♭maj7 B♭m7 E♭7(♭9) A♭maj7
— Walk my way and a thou - sand vi - o - lins be - gin to play, or it might be the
A♭m D♭9 E♭maj7 Cm Fm7 B♭7(♭9)
sound of your hel - lo, that mu - sic I hear, I get mist - y, the mo - ment you're
E♭ Cm7 Fm7 B♭7(♭9) E♭6 Ddim E♭6 B♭m7
near. You can say that you're lead - ing me on,
E♭7(♭9) A♭maj7 A♭6 B♭dim A♭6
— but it's just what I want you to do. Don't you no - tice how

Am7 D7 F7 B♭ Edim Fm7 B♭7(♭9) B♭9
3
hope - less - ly I'm lost, that's why I'm fol - low - ing you. On my
E♭maj7 B♭m7 E♭7(♭9) A♭maj7
fr5
3 3
own, would I wan - der through this won - der - land a - lone, nev - er know - ing my
A♭m D♭9 E♭maj7 Cm Fm7 B♭7(♭9)
fr5 fr5
3 3 3
right foot from my left, my hat from my glove, I'm too mist - y and too much in
1. E♭ E9 Fm7 B♭7(♯5) B♭9
2. E♭ A♭maj7 Gm7 E7 E♭maj7
fr5 fr5 fr5 fr5
mf
love. Look at love.

THE MORE I SEE YOU

Betty Grable and Dick Haymes were the stars of the 1945 film Billy Rose's Diamond Horseshoe, *and their duet of this lovely ballad was included in the movie. Dick Haymes had the hit recording of the song that same year, followed closely by a version from Harry James and his orchestra.*

Betty Grable

Words by MACK GORDON
Music by HARRY WARREN

Refrain, with feeling
Fm7 Ebdim Eb Bb7 Eb Ebmaj7 Fm7 Bb7 Fm7 Ebdim
The more I see you, the more I want you. Some - how this
Eb Bb7 Eb Edim Fm7 Bb7 Fm7 Bb7
feel - ing just grows and grows. With ev - 'ry
Ebm Bb Dbm Gb7 Cb Abm7 Bb7+5
sigh I be - come more mad a - bout you; more lost with -
Ebm F9 Fm7 Bb7 Fm7 Bb Fm7 Ebdim
out you, and so it goes. Can you im -

Eb
Bb7
Eb
Ebmaj7
Fm7
Bb7
Fm7
Ebdim
ag - ine how much I'll love you, the more I
Eb
Bb7
Eb
Bb+
Bbm7
Eb7
Bbm7
Eb7
Dbm
Bbdim
Ab
see you as years go by? I know the on - ly one for
Abm
Eb
C7
F7
Eb
Fm7
Fdim
me can on - ly be you. My arms won't free you, my heart won't
1.
Eb
Fm7
Ebdim
2.
Eb
Ab9
Eb
try. The more I try.

Perry Como

MORE THAN YOU KNOW

Premiered by Mayo Methot in the 1929 musical Great Day, *"More Than You Know" has been performed by such venerable arists as Ruth Etting (1930), Mildred Bailey (1937), Benny Goodman (1935), Perry Como (1946) and Jane Froman. It was later featured in the films* Hit The Deck *(1955),* Funny Lady *(1975) and an episode of ABC's television series* Life Goes On, *by Patti Lupone.*

Words by
WILLIAM ROSE and EDWARD ELISCU
Music by
VINCENT YOUMANS

Moderately

mf

Ebm Ebm6 D7+5 Ebm Ebm6

Wheth - er you are here or yon - der, wheth-er you are false or

Fm7-5/Cb Bb7 Ebm Gb7 Cbmaj7 Fm7-5

true, wheth - er you re - main or wan - der I'm grow - ing

Ebm/Bb
A°
Bb7
Ebm
Ebm6
fond - er of you. E - ven though your friends for -
D7+5
Ebm
Ebm6
sake you, e - ven though you don't suc -
Fm7-5/C
Bb7
Ebm
Gb7
ceed, would - n't I be glad to
Cbmaj7
Fm7-5
Ebm/Bb
Bb°7
Ab/Bb
Bb7+5
take you, give you the break you need. More than you

Eb6
Bb7+5
Eb9
Abmaj7
C7-9
know, more than you know, man o' my heart, I love you
Ab6
Ab7
Bb7
F7/A
Bb7sus4
Bb9
so. Late - ly I find you're on my mind, more than you
Ebmaj7
Dbmaj7
Bb7
Bb7+5
Eb6
Bb7+5
know. Wheth - er you're right, wheth - er you're
Eb9
Abmaj7
C7-9
Ab6
Db7
wrong, man o' my heart I'll string a - long. You need me

Gm7 C7 F7 B♭7 E♭ Fm7
3fr.
so more than you'll ev - er know.
Gm7 Am7-5 D7 Gm
3fr.
Lov - ing you the way that I do there's
Cm Dm7 Gm Cm7-5
3fr.
noth - ing I can do a - bout it,
lov - ing may be
B♭/F Gm7 C7 F7
3fr.
all you can give but hon - ey I can't live with -

Bb7
Bbo7
Bb11
Bb7+5
6fr.
Eb6
Bb7+5
6fr.
out it. Oh, how I'd cry, oh, how I'd
Eb9
Abmaj7
4fr.
C7-9
Ab6
Db7
4fr.
cry, if you got tired and said "good - bye," more than I'd
Gm7
3fr.
C7
F11
Bb9
1.
Eb
Ao7
show more than you'd ev - er know.
Bb7/F
Bb7+5
6fr.
2.Eb
Db7
4fr.
Ebmaj7
More than you know.

Frank Sinatra, Bing Crosby and Dean Martin in *Robin And The Seven Hoods*

MY KIND OF TOWN

(Chicago Is)

We had to write a song about Chicago for the film Robin And The Seven Hoods, *and I knew there was a great Chicago song called "Chicago," so to protect the original copyright and create a new copyright we called our song "My Kind Of Town." I wish more of the new writers would understand what I am insinuating—don't repeat titles!*

Words by
SAMMY CAHN
Music by
JAMES VAN HEUSEN

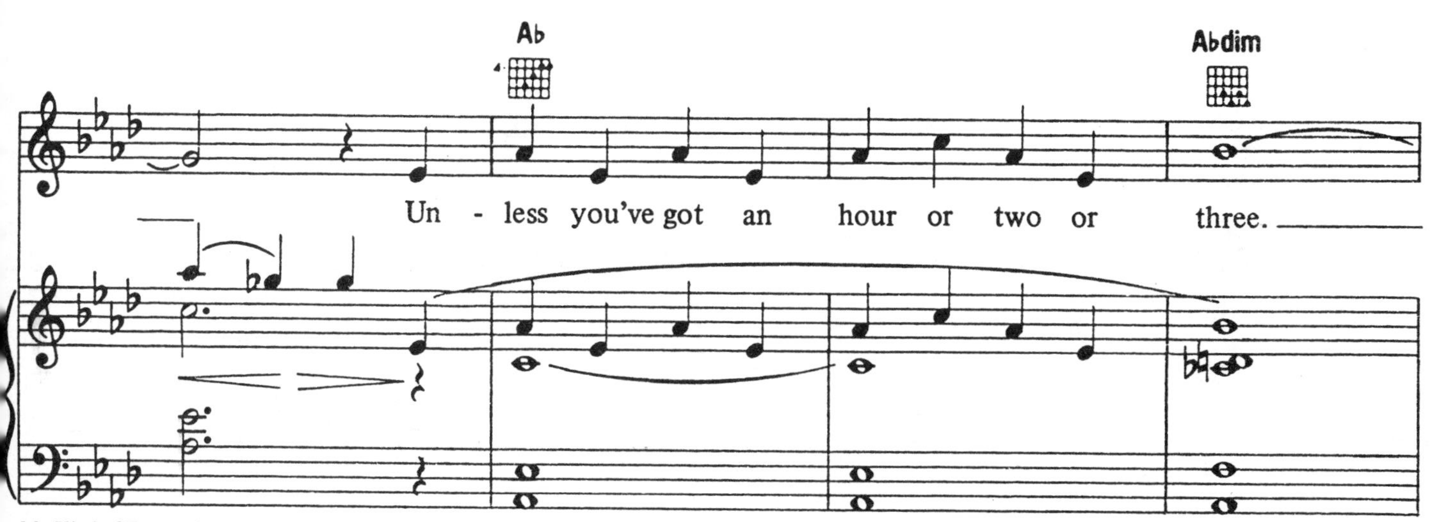

*) Any city name of three syllables can replace Chicago, such as Manhattan, Las Vegas, etc.

Ab Edim Fm Bb9 Gm Bb7 Eb9 Ebdim
peo - ple, too, Peo - ple who smile at
razz - ma-tazz, And it has that there
Eb9 G7 Ab G7 Gb9 F7 F9 F7+(b9) F7
you and each time I roam, Chi - ca - go is,
jazz and each time I leave, Chi - ca - go is,
Bbm Ebdim Eb7 Ab Abdim Ab7 C7-5
call - ing me home,
tug - ging my sleeve,
Chi - ca - go is,
1. Db6 Ddim Ab Ab7 F7+ F7 Bb9
One town that won't let you down, It's My

(1.)
Bbm9
Eb13-9
Ab6
Abdim
Ab6
Kind Of Town!
Bbm7
F7
Bbm7
Abdim
2. Db6
Ddim
This is The Wrig - ley
Ab
Abdim
Ab
C7-5
Db6
Ddim
Build - ing, Chi - ca - go is, The Wind - y
Ab
Abdim
Ab
C7-5
Db6
Ddim
Cit - y, Chi - ca - go is, The Un - ion

Ab Abdim Ab C7-5 Db6 Ddim

Stock-yards, Chi - ca - go is, Com - isk - ey

Ab Abdim Ab C7-5 Db6 Ddim

Ball - park, Chi - ca - go is, One town that

cresc.

Ab Ab7 F7+ F7 Bb9 Bbm7

won't let you down, It's My Kind

Eb13-9 Ab6 E7-5 Eb9 Ab6 (9)

Of Town!

Paul Anka

MY WAY

Paul Anka wrote the English version of this song (originally "Comme d'Habitude" in France) specifically for Sinatra, and who can think of "My Way" any way but his way? Even Elvis "The King of Rock & Roll" Presley's gold record version can't compare to the Chairman of the Board's.

English Words by
PAUL ANKA
Music by
JACQUES REVAUX and CLAUDE FRANCOIS
Original French Words by
GILES THIBAULT

Moderately slow

C Em Dm7 G7

mf

And

C Em/B Gm6/B♭ A7

now the end is near, and so I face the fin - al cur - tain. My
grets, I've had a few, but then a - gain, too few to men - tion. I

Dm Dm7 G7 C

friend, I'll say it clear, I'll state my case, of which I'm cer - tain. I've
did what I had to do, and saw it through with - out ex - emp - tion. I

C7
F
Fm
lived a life that's full, I trav-eled each and ev-'ry high-way. And
planned each chart-ered course, each care-ful step a-long the by-way. And
C
G7
1.
F6
C
2.
F6
more, much more than this, I did it my way. Re-my
more, much more than this, I did it
C
C
C7
F
way. Yes, there were times, I'm sure you knew, when I bit off more than I could
Dm7
G7
Em7
chew. But through it all, when there was doubt, I ate it up, and spit it

Am
Dm7
G7
C
out. I faced it all, and I stood tall, and did it my way. I've
C
Em/B
Gm6/B♭
A7
loved, I've laughed and cried, I've had my fill, my share of los - ing. And
Dm
Dm7
G7
C
now, as tears sub - side, I find it all so a - mus - ing. To
C7
F
Fm
think I did all that, and may I say, "Not in a shy way." Oh,

C
G7
F6
C
no, oh no, not me, I did it my way. For what is a
C
C7
F
man, what has he got, if not him - self, then he has not to say the
Dm7
G7
Em7
Am
things he tru - ly feels, and not the words of one who kneels. The rec - ord
Dm7
G7
C
shows I took the blows, and did it my way.
rit.

Frank Sinatra

NICE 'N' EASY

Although a staple in the repertoire of just about every jazz great, many still treasure Frank Sinatra's 1960 recording. It's available on the gold album Nice 'N' Easy *(Capitol 1417) which, incidentally, logged nine weeks in the no. 1 spot.*

Words by
ALAN and MARILYN BERGMAN
Music by
LEW SPENCE

Slow

mf

C C+ C6 C7 Dm7

Refrain

mp–mf

take it Nice 'N' Eas - y It's gon - na be so eas - y For us to fall

Gdim G7 C C+

— in love. Hey, ba - by, what's your hur - ry?

C6 C7 Dm7 A7(-9) Dm Dm7

Re - lax and don't you wor - ry, We're gon - na fall in love.

Dm6
E7(-9)
Am
C+
C
G7
C
Gm6
We're on the road to ro - mance, that's safe to say, But let's make all the stops
A7
A7(+5)
D7
Dm7
G7(-9)
C
C+
C6
a-long the way. The prob-lem now, of course is To sim-ply
C7
F
E7
Am
Am7
D9
4fr.
E♭dim
C
Am7
hold your hors - es, To rush would be a crime 'cause Nice 'N' Eas - y
Dm7
G9
G7(-9)
1. C
Em7
Dm7
G9
2. C
Am7
Dm7
D♭7
C6
does it ev - 'ry time! time!

OLD DEVIL MOON

This delightful song is from Finian's Rainbow, *a 1947 Broadway musical. The show, about a leprechaun and a pot of gold, ran for 725 performances. It was later made into a film musical starring Fred Astaire and Petula Clark.*

Words by
E.Y. HARBURG

Music by
BURTON LANE

Abm
Db7
Gb
C7
F
C7
To Coda
Old Dev - il Moon in your eyes.
Old Dev - il Moon in your eyes,
mf
F
Eb
F
Eb
D
F#m
You and your glance makes this ro - mance too hot to han - dle.
mp
D
Dm
F+
Dm7
G7
C7
Bb
Stars in the night blaz - ing their light Can't hold a can - dle
Ebm
D.S. al Coda
to your raz - zle daz - zle.
CODA
F
Eb
F
Eb
Just when I think I'm free as a
F
C7
Eb
F
Eb
F
Eb
F
dove Old Dev-il Moon deep in your eyes blinds me with love.
mf
L.H.
f

ON A CLEAR DAY (YOU CAN SEE FOREVER)

From the 1965 Broadway musical of the same name, this song has become one of the great modern standards, recorded by dozens of performers. This show was made into a film musical starring Barbra Streisand.

Lyrics by
ALAN JAY LERNER

Music by
BURTON LANE

Dm7/G G7 Dm7 G7
star. You feel part of ev- 'ry moun-tain, sea and shore. You can
mf più espr.
Cmaj7 Dm6 A7 D7 Edim Gmaj7
hear, from far and near, a world you've nev- er heard be- fore. And on a clear day,
G Bm7 E9 Bm E9 Am7 G6 Am7 G6
1. Am7 D7
On that clear day You can see for- ev- er and ev- er-
cresc.
G Em Am7 D7
more!
2. Am7 G6 Am7 G6 Am7
On a ev- er and ev- er and ev-
mp
p poco rit.
D7 G Em9 Am9 D7 Gmaj7 G
er- more!
mf
accel.
p

OVER THE RAINBOW

Perhaps the most beloved of all standards, it is from the classic film The Wizard of Oz. *Sung by Judy Garland before the tornado whisks her off to the magical land of Oz, the song was almost cut from the film, as MGM mogul Louis B. Mayer felt it slowed down the action.*

Lyric by
E.Y. HARBURG

Music by
HAROLD ARLEN

Cm
Ab7
F9
Fm7
Eb
Lead - ing from your win - dow pane. To a place be-hind the
Fm7
Eb
Ebdim
Fm7
Bb7
sun, Just a step be-yond the rain.
rall.
Chorus Moderately (not fast)
Eb
Gm
Eb7
Ab
Abmaj7
Ab7
Gm7
Eb
Gm7
Edim
Some - where O - ver The Rain - bow way up high,
p - mf
Ab6
Abm6
Eb
C-9
F7
Fm
Bb7
Eb
Fm7
Bb-9
There's a land that I heard of once in a lull - a - by,

Eb
Gm
Eb7
Ab
Abmaj7
Ab7
Gm7
Eb
Gm7
Edim
Ab6
Abm6
Some - where O - ver The Rain-bow skies are blue, And the
Eb
C-9
F7
Fm
Bb7
Eb
dreamily
Eb
Eb6
Eb
dreams that you dare to dream real - ly do come true. Some-day I'll wish up-on a star and
Fm7
Bb7
Eb6
Bb
Ab
Eb
Bb7
Eb
Eb
Eb
wake up where the clouds are far be-hind me, Where troub-les melt like lem-on drops, a-
Cdim
Fm6
Ebm
Cdim
Fm7
Bb9+
Eb
-way, a - bove the chim-ney tops that's where you'll find me. Some - where

Gm Eb7 Ab Abmaj7 Ab7 Gm7 Eb Gm7 Edim Ab6 Abm6

O - ver The Rain - bow blue - birds fly, Birds fly

Eb C-9 F7 Fm Bb7 1. Eb Bb9 Bb-9 2. Eb

O - ver The Rain - bow, why then, oh why can't I? I?

rall.

Guitar Tacit

If

Eb Fm7 Bb7 Eb6

hap - py lit - tle blue - birds fly be - yond the rain - bow, why oh why can't I?

rit. *pp*

l.h. *ten.*

THE PARTY'S OVER

This song was first introduced by the great Judy Holliday in 1956 in the Broadway musical Bells Are Ringing. *Several years later it was made into a musical starring Ms. Holliday and Dean Martin.*

Words by
BETTY COMDEN and ADOLPH GREEN

Music by
JULE STYNE

C7 F7 Bb7 Ab Bb7 Eb Ab Bb7 Eb

must be paid. The par- ty's o- ver, The can- dles flick- er and dim.

Ab Bb7 Eb Ab Eb Ab Db F#m

You danced and dreamed through the night, It seemed to be right, Just be- ing with him.

cresc.

Eb7 Eb7+5 Ab6 C#m Bb7 Bbm6 C7

Now you must wake up, All dreams must end. Take off your

mf

Fm Db7 Bb7 Ab Bb7 Ebmaj7 Cm Fm7

make- up, The par- ty's o- ver, It's all o- ver,

Bb7 1. Eb Ebdim Fm7 Bb7 2. Eb Fm7 Abm6 Eb6

my friend. The par- ty's friend.

rit. *f*

Gene Kelly and Leslie Caron in *An American In Paris (1951 film version)*

'S WONDERFUL

The Gershwins' score for their 1927 musical comedy, Funny Face, *is highlighted by this memorable number, where Ira cleverly used elision to join together and shorten words. The song was introduced by Allen Kearns and Adele Astaire in the show, and Fred Astaire and Audrey Hepburn performed it nearly 30 years later in the film version.*

Music and Lyrics by
GEORGE GERSHWIN and IRA GERSHWIN

Moderato
mf

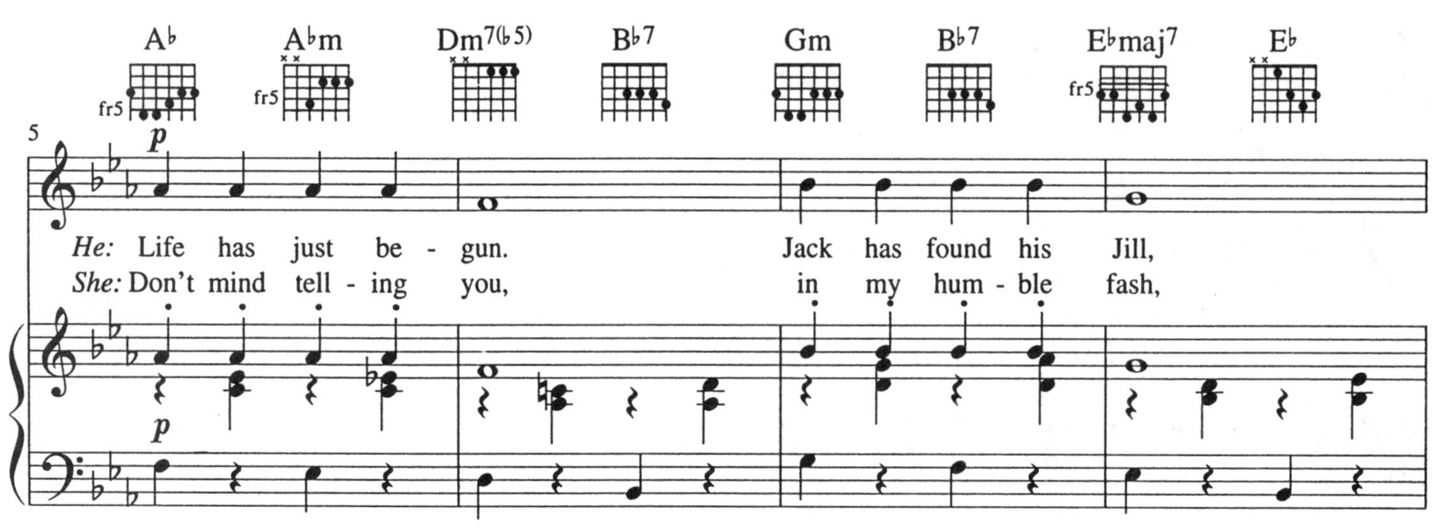
A♭
A♭m
Dm7(♭5)
B♭7
Gm
B♭7
E♭maj7
E♭
fr5
p
He: Life has just be - gun. Jack has found his Jill,
She: Don't mind tell - ing you, in my hum - ble fash,

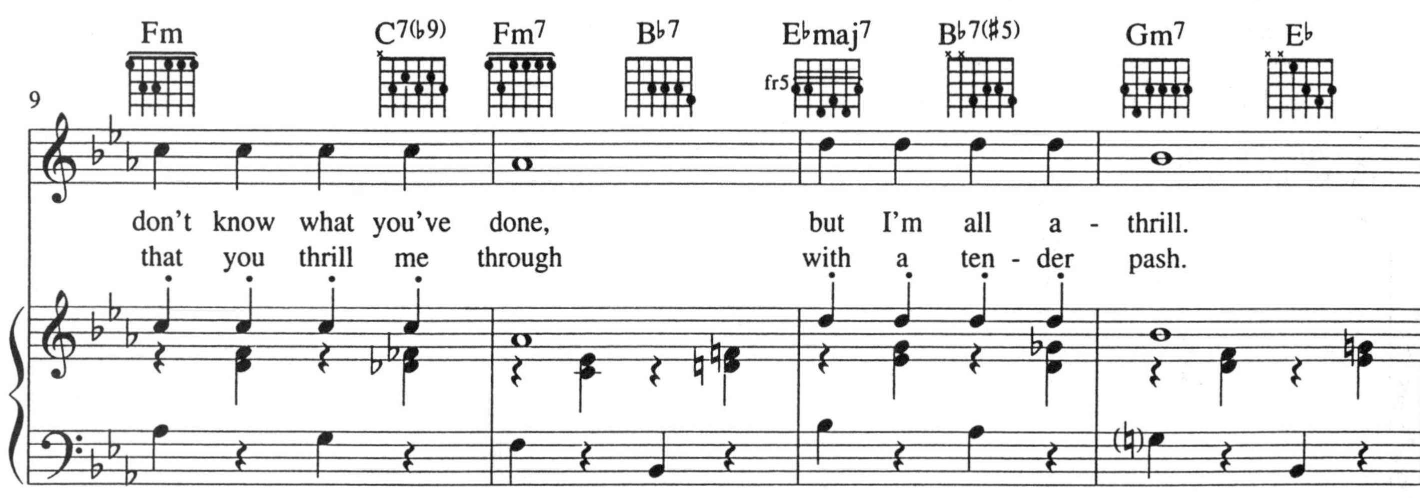
Fm
C7(♭9)
Fm7
B♭7
E♭maj7
B♭7(♯5)
Gm7
E♭
fr5
don't know what you've done, but I'm all a - thrill.
that you thrill me through with a ten - der pash.

Cm
E♭
Am7(♭5)
D7
Gm
B♭7(♯5)
Gm7(♭5)
C7
How can words ex - press your di - vine ap - peal?
When you said you care, 'mag - ine my e - mosh;
Fm
C
Fm7(♭5)
B♭
E♭
B♭
B♭dim7
C7
You can nev - er guess all the love I feel.
I swore then and there per - ma - nent de - vosh.
B♭
F9
F7
B♭
D♭m6
G♭7
B♭
fr5
From now on la - dy I in - sist, for me no
You made all oth - er boys seem blah; just you a -
F9
F7
Fm7
A♭m
B♭7
Refrain:
E♭
E♭6
E♭
E♭6
fr5
un poco rit.
p – mf a tempo
oth - er girls ex - ist.
lone filled me with Aah!
'S won - der - ful!

C7
C♯dim7
C7
C♯dim7
B♭7(6)
B♭7
'S mar - vel - ous!
You should care for
E♭6
E♭
E♭6
E♭
E♭6
E♭
E♭6
me!
'S aw - ful nice
C7
C♯dim7
C7
C♯dim7
B♭6
B♭7
'S par - a - dise!
'S what I love to
E♭6
Am7(♭5)
G
D7
see!
You've made my life so
My dear, it's four - leaf
mf

47 G D7 Dm6 C7

cresc.

glam - or - ous ____ you can't blame me for feel - ing
clo - ver time, ____ from now on my heart's work - ing

cresc.

51 F7 B♭7 E♭ E♭6 E♭ E♭6

p

am - o - rous. ____ Oh! 'S won - der - ful! ____
o - ver - time. ____

p

55 Cm F7 F Fm7 Edim7 Fm7 B♭7

mf *p*

'S mar - vel - ous! ____ That you should care ____ for

mf *p*

59 1. E♭ Gm Fm A♭ Gm Cm Fm7 B♭ 2. E♭ A♭ E♭

fr5

me! me! ____

mf *dim.* *mf*

SEPTEMBER IN THE RAIN

This haunting reverie of a September worth remembering was first performed by opera tenor James Melton in the 1937 film Melody for Two. *It went on to become a melody for many; more than 17 different recordings of this song have since been released by artists, including Bing Crosby, Frank Sinatra, The Platters and Nelson Riddle and his orchestra.*

Words by
AL DUBIN
Music by
HARRY WARREN

Light swing beat

Bb7+5 Eb Gm7 Cm Gm7 Fm
mf
The leaves of brown came tumbling down, remember?
sun went out just like a dying ember

Fm-5 Bb7 1. Eb
In September, in the rain.
that September, in the

Bb7+5 2. Eb
The rain To

Bbm7 Eb7 Bbm7 Eb7 Ab6 Abmaj7
ev - 'ry word of love I heard you whis - per,
Ab6 Cm7 3 fr. F7 2 fr. Cm7 3 fr. F7 2 fr.
the rain - drops seemed to play a sweet re -
Bb7 Fm 7 Bb7 Fm7 Bb7 Bb7+5 Eb 3fr. Gm7
frain. Though spring is here, to
Cm 3 fr. Gm7 Fm Fm-5
me it's still Sep - tem - ber, that Sep - tem - ber
Bb7 Eb 3fr. Eb6/9
in the rain.

Ella Fitzgerald

SOMEBODY LOVES ME

The men responsible for this song had amazing careers. This song was Gershwin's third big hit of 1924, following the successes of "Rhapsody in Blue" and "Fascinating Rhythm." Lyricist B.G. "Buddy" DeSylva went on to become a notable Broadway and film producer, as well as head of Paramount Pictures. Considered a Gershwin classic, "Somebody Loves Me" has been recorded by the greatest names in show business: Dinah Washington, Ella Fitzgerald, Maynard Ferguson, Harry James and Nat "King" Cole, to name just a few.

Words by B.G. DeSYLVA and BALLARD MacDONALD
Music by GEORGE GERSHWIN

Allegro moderato

mf

Em F♯m Bm Em6 Em F♯m Bm Em6

mp

When this world be - gan it was Heav - en's plan

F♯m7 B7sus4 B7 Em7 Em6 Am6 B7 Em

There should be a girl for ev - 'ry man.

G Am D7 G6 G Am D7 G6

To my great re - gret some - one has up - set

Am7
D7sus4
D7
G7
G7/C
Em/C
Cm6
D7
Em
Em6
Heav - en's pret - ty pro - gram for we've nev - er met. I'm
Bm
Bm6
E7
Em7
A7
D7
D+
clutch - ing at straws, just be - cause I may meet her yet.
poco rit.
Refrain:
G
Am7
Am
D7
G
Some - bod - y loves me I won - der
p - f a tempo (molto legato)
C7
G
C7
Am7
D7
who, I won - der who she can be.

G
D7-9
G
Some - bod - y
Am7
Am
D7
G
A7
loves me I wish I knew,
Bm
C♯7-9
C♯m7
F♯7
Bm
Who can she be wor - ries me.
E7
Am
Dm6
Am
Dm6
For ev - 'ry girl who pass - es me I shout, hey!

Am6
Em7
A7
Em7
A7
May - be you were meant to be my lov - ing
D7
D+
G
Am7
Am
D7
ba - by. Some - bod - y loves me
G
C7
3
G
Em7
Am7
D7
I won - der who, may - be it's
1.
G
you.
mf
2.
G
Am
G
you.
rit. e dim.
fz

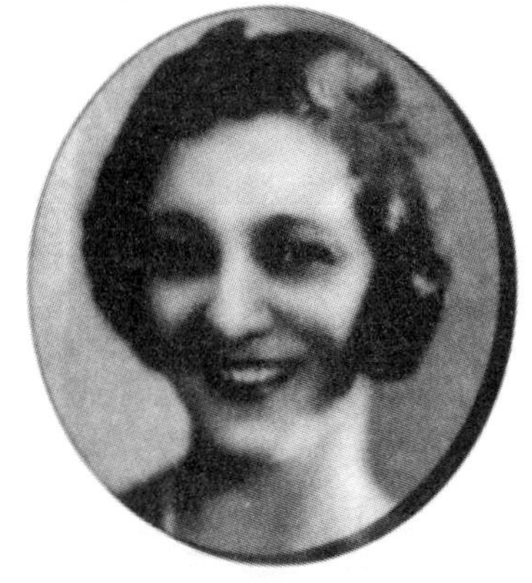

SOMEONE TO WATCH OVER ME

Gertrude Lawrence

Gertrude Lawrence made her American debut in Gershwin's Oh Kay!, *which introduced this timeless favorite. The song was first popularized by George Olsen and his orchestra and was later performed by Frank Sinatra in 1942's* Young At Heart. *Other films featuring this luminous melody include the 1946 Gershwin biography,* Rhapsody In Blue, *1955's* Three For The Show *(performed by Marge and Gower Champion) and 1957's* Beau James, *as sing by Vera Miles.*

Music and Lyrics by
GEORGE GERSHWIN and IRA GERSHWIN

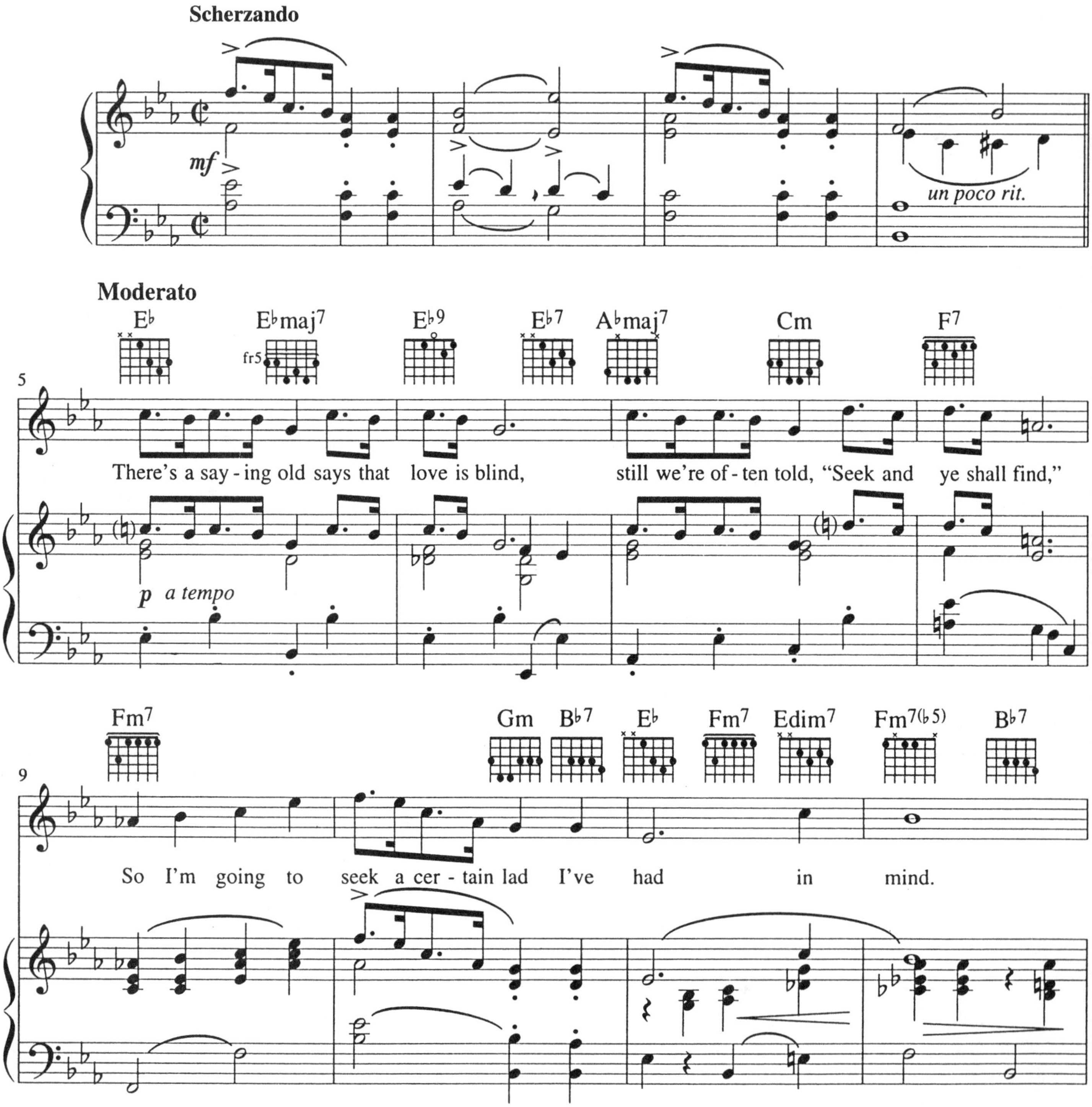

Scherzando
mf
un poco rit.
Moderato
E♭
E♭maj7
fr5
E♭9
E♭7
A♭maj7
Cm
F7
5
There's a say - ing old says that love is blind, still we're of - ten told, "Seek and ye shall find,"
p a tempo
Fm7
Gm
B♭7
E♭
Fm7
Edim7
Fm7(♭5)
B♭7
9
So I'm going to seek a cer - tain lad I've had in mind.

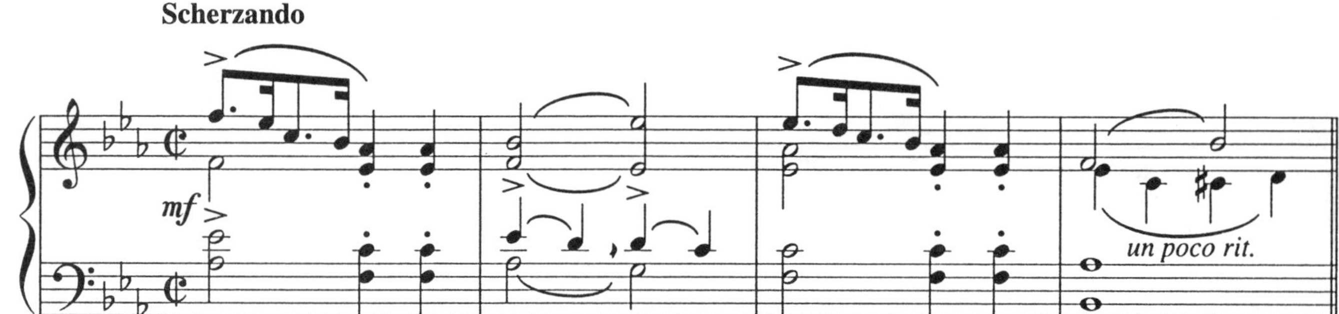

E♭ E♭maj7 E♭9 E♭7 A♭maj7 Cm F7
13
Look - ing ev - 'ry - where, have - n't found him yet; He's the big af - fair I can - not for - get.
Fm7 Gm B♭7 E♭ A♭ E♭ D7(♭9)
17
On - ly man I ev - er think of with re - gret.
Gm C Gm C7
21
mp
I'd like to add his i - ni - tial to my mon - o - gram.
B♭ B♭6 Cm7 F7 B♭ A♭ Gm B♭7
25
mf
un poco rall.
Tell me, where is the shep - herd for this lost lamb?

E♭
E♭7
A♭6
A♭dim7
E♭
E♭dim7
B♭7
B♭dim7
a tempo
There's a some - bod - y I'm long - ing to see. I hope that he turns out to be
a tempo
Fm
C7
Fm
Am7(♭5)
Fm7
B♭7
E♭
G7(♯5)
A♭
B♭7
E♭
E♭7
fr5
some - one who'll watch o - ver me.
I'm a lit - tle lamb who's
A♭6
A♭dim7
E♭
E♭dim7
B♭7
B♭dim7
Fm
C7
Fm
lost in the wood. I know I could al - ways be good to one who'll
Am7(♭5)
Fm7
B♭7
E♭
E♭7
A♭
B♭7
E♭
A♭
fr5
watch o - ver me. Al - though he may not be the

46
E♭ D7 D7(♯5) D7 G7
man some girls think of as hand - some. To my heart he car - ries the
51
C C7 F7 B♭7 E♭ E♭7 A♭6 A♭dim7
p
key. Won't you tell him please to put on some speed,
55
E♭ E♭dim7 B♭7 B♭dim7 Fm C7 Fm Am7(♭5) Fm7 B♭7
fr5
fol - low my lead, oh, how I need some - one to watch o - ver
59
1. E♭ E♭7 A♭ G7(♯5) Fm7 B♭7(♯5)
2. E♭ E♭7 A♭ A♭m E♭
me. me.
mf

SOMETIMES I'M HAPPY

With lyrics by Oscar Hammerstein II and William Cary Duncan and music by Vincent Youmans, "Come On And Pet Me" should have been good enough for any show, but it was dropped anyway from 1923's Mary Jane McKane. *Youmans almost never gave up on a tune, however, and turned it over to Irving Caesar for new lyrics (and a new title). Two years later, Louise Groody and Charles King sang "Sometimes I'm Happy" in* Hit The Deck *and finally hit the mark. It was featured in both film versions of* Hit The Deck *(with performances by Polly Walker and Jack Oakie in 1930, and Jane Powell and Vic Damone in the 1955 remake).*

Words by
IRVING CAESAR

Music by
VINCENT YOUMANS

Sometimes I'm Happy - 3 - 1

A
Em/A
C#o7
D
Do7
D
Bm7-5
I nev - er mind the rain from the skies,
A
E+5
A
Em
F#7
B7
If I can find the sun in your eyes.
E7
A
E9
Some - times I love you,
A
E7
A
some - times I hate you, but when I

E9
A
E7
hate you,
It's 'cause I love___ you.
A
Em/A
C♯°7
D
D°7
D
Bm7-5
That's how I am, so what can I do?___
A
Bm7
E7
I'm hap - py when I'm with
A
A6
B9
B♭9
A9
you.___

Sinatra with Count Basie

(Love Is)
THE TENDER TRAP

James Van Heusen (born Edward Chester Babcock) and Sammy Cahn are among the most respected songwriters of the 1900's. Theirs are the creative minds responsible for Academy Award winning songs "High Hopes" (1959), and "Call Me Irresponsible" (1963). Most of this duo's hits are from films, and "The Tender Trap" is no exception. Taken from the movie of the same name, Frank Sinatra's Capitol recording reached no. 7 on the Billboard pop chart in 1955. (This Is Sinatra, *Capitol 11883;* Sinatra-Basie, *Reprise FS1008)*

Words by
SAMMY CAHN

Music by
JAMES VAN HEUSEN

Moderato

mf

Refrain: C7 F F♯°7 Cm7

You see a pair of laugh-ing eyes And sud-den-ly you're sigh-ing sighs,

mp - mf

C7 Cm7 F9 B♭maj7 B♭6

You're think-ing noth-ing's wrong, you string a-long, boy, then

A7+5
D7
Am7
Dm
D7
G9
ff
snap!
Those eyes, those sighs, They're part
Gm7
C7-9
F
G9
C7 6
C7-5
C7
of The Ten - der Trap!
You're
F
F♯°7
Cm7
hand in hand be - neath the trees
And soon there's mu - sic in the breeze,

C7
Cm7
F9
B♭maj7
B♭6
You're act - ing kind of smart, un - til your heart just goes
A7+5
D7
Am7
Dm
D7
G9
whap!
Those trees, that breeze, They're part
ff
Gm7
C7-9
F
Gm7
F°7
F
F°
of the Ten - der Trap!
Some star - ry

Em7-5
A7
Dm
Gm
night, when {her his} kiss - es make you tin - gle,
Dm
D°7
Em7-5
A7
{She'll He'll} hold you tight and you'll hate your - self for
Dm
G7/6
Gm7
G♭7
C7
F
be - ing sin - gle. And all at once it seems so nice,

F♯o7
Cm7
C7
The folks are throw-ing shoes and rice,
You
Cm7
F9
B♭maj7
B♭6
A7+5
hur-ry to a spot, that's just a dot on the map!
ff
D7
Am7
Dm
D7
G9
Gm7
C7
You won-der how it all came a-bout, It's too

Am7-5
Cm
F7
Cm
D7
C
D7
D7+5
late now, there's no get - ting out, You fell
Gm
Gm(maj7)
Gm7
C7 6
G♭7
F
1.
D7-5 -9
Gm7
in love and love is The Ten - der Trap!
C7-5 -9
2.
G♭7
Fmaj7
G♭6 F6
You

Charles Chaplin

THIS IS MY SONG

Comedic genius Charles Chaplin was also a fine songwriter; his output included "Smile," "Eternally," and film scores for City Lights, The Great Dictator, Modern Times, *and many others. This theme from the 1965 movie* The Countess From Hong Kong, *was contested by French composer Charles Trenet as being identical to the opening bars of his 1941 song, "Romance of Paris." Petula Clark's vocal rendition was a major hit record in 1967.*

Words and Music by
CHARLES CHAPLIN

Barcarolle

Verse

F

Why is my heart so light?
Flow-ers are smil - ing bright

p

Gm7 C7

Why are the stars so bright? Why is the sky so
Smil - ing for our de - light, Smil - ing so ten - der -

Gm7 C7 F

blue ___ since the hour ___ I met you? ___ A - lone I sing in
ly ___ for the world ___ you and me. ___ I know why the world is

C9
C7
F
moon - light with you in my heart su - preme To
smil - ing, smil - ing so ten - der - ly; It
D7
Gm
Gm7
C7
hear you say I love you That is my hope my dream.
hears the same old sto - ry Through-out e - ter - ni - ty.
Chorus
Rubato
F
C7
Love This Is My Song Here is a song, a ser - e-nade to you The

Gm
C7
F
world can-not be wrong If in this world there's you I
Gm
C7
F
care not what the world may say With-out your love there is no day
Gm7
C9
Love This Is My Song Here is a song, a ser-e-nade to
1.F
2.F
you.
you.
p
molto rit.

Pictured here with Jule Styne and Sammy Kahn, Ol' Blue Eyes receives a special "Pied Piper" Award from ASCAP (American Society of Composers, Authors and Publishers.)

TIME AFTER TIME

Jule Styne was one of Sammy Cahn's chief collaborators. He composed the 1954 Academy Award winning song "Three Coins In The Fountain," which was sung by Sinatra on the soundtrack for that film. He is also responsible for numerous other hits from Broadway shows and from films. "Time After Time," a song describing unending love and adoration, was introduced by Frank Sinatra in the 1947 film It Happened In Brooklyn. *(*This Is Frank Sinatra Vol. 2, *Capitol DN16268;* In The Beginning, *Columbia PG31358)*

Words by
SAMMY CAHN
Music by
JULE STYNE

Moderato

mf

F G G9 C E♭°7

What good are words I say to you? They can't con-

mp

Dm7 G7 G9 G7-9 C

vey to you what's in my heart. If you could

Am
Am7
D7
F°7
C
G7
C
hear in - stead the things I've
mf
Am
Am7
D7
F°7
C
Eb7
Dm7
Db9-5
left un - said!
rit.
Chorus
C
Am
Dm7
G7
C
Em
Dm7
G7
TIME AF-TER TIME I tell my-self that I'm so
Know what I know the pass-ing years will show you've
mp
a tempo

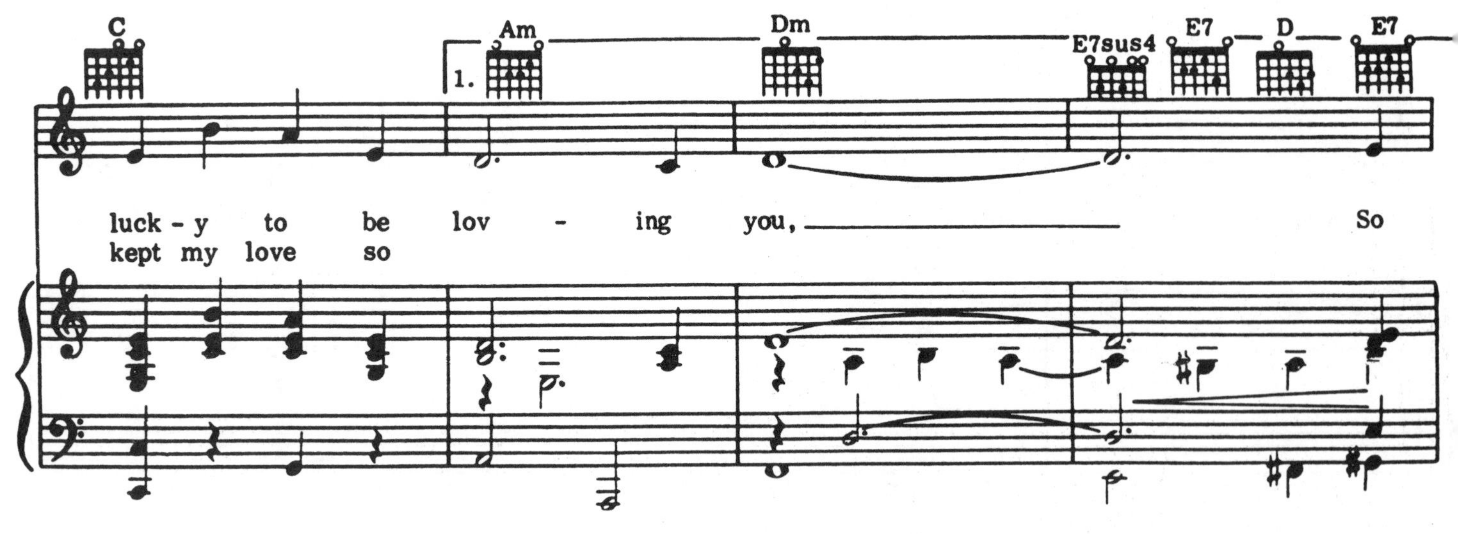
C
Am
Dm
E7sus4
E7
D
E7
1.
luck - y to be lov - ing you, So
kept my love so

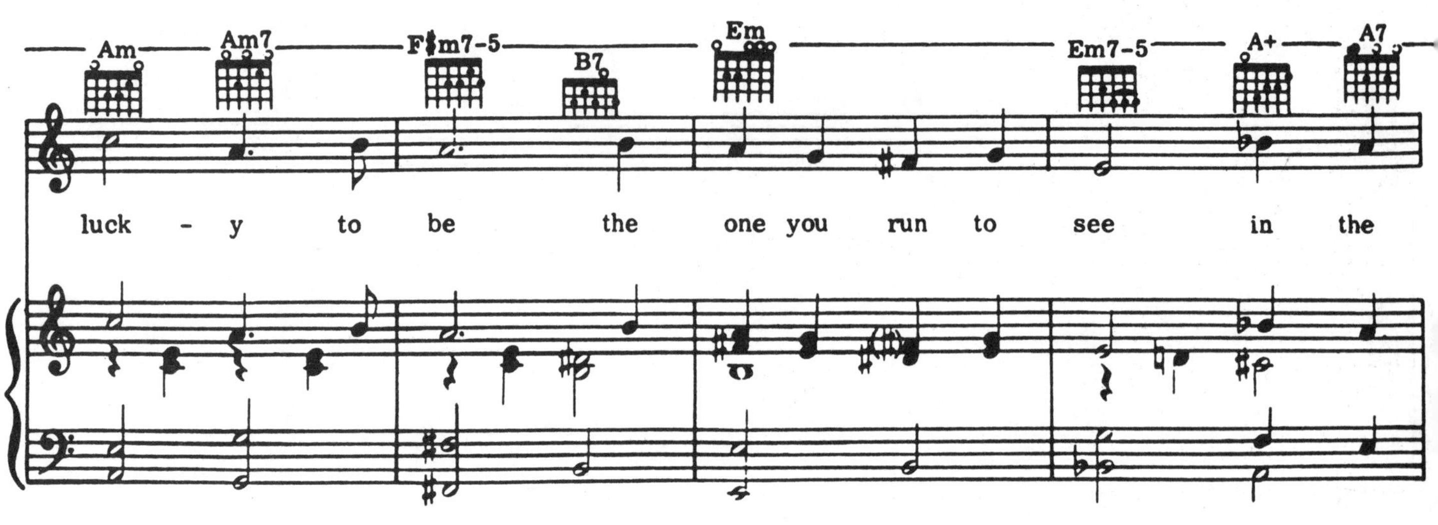
Am
Am7
F♯m7-5
B7
Em
Em7-5
A+
A7
luck - y to be the one you run to see in the

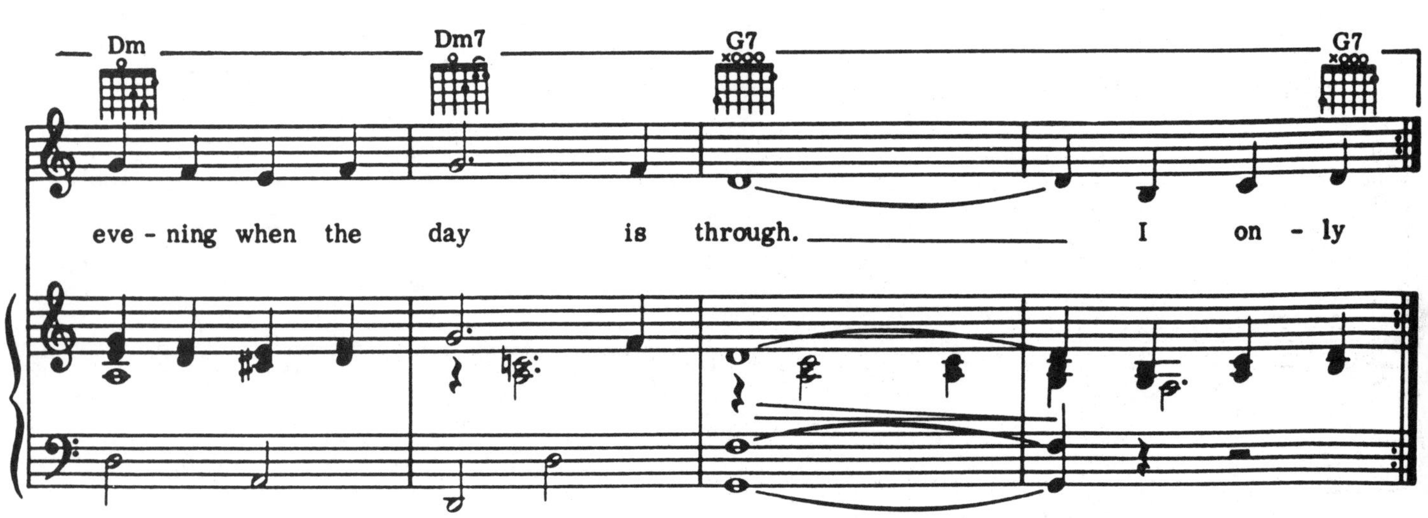
Dm
Dm7
G7
G7
eve - ning when the day is through. I on - ly

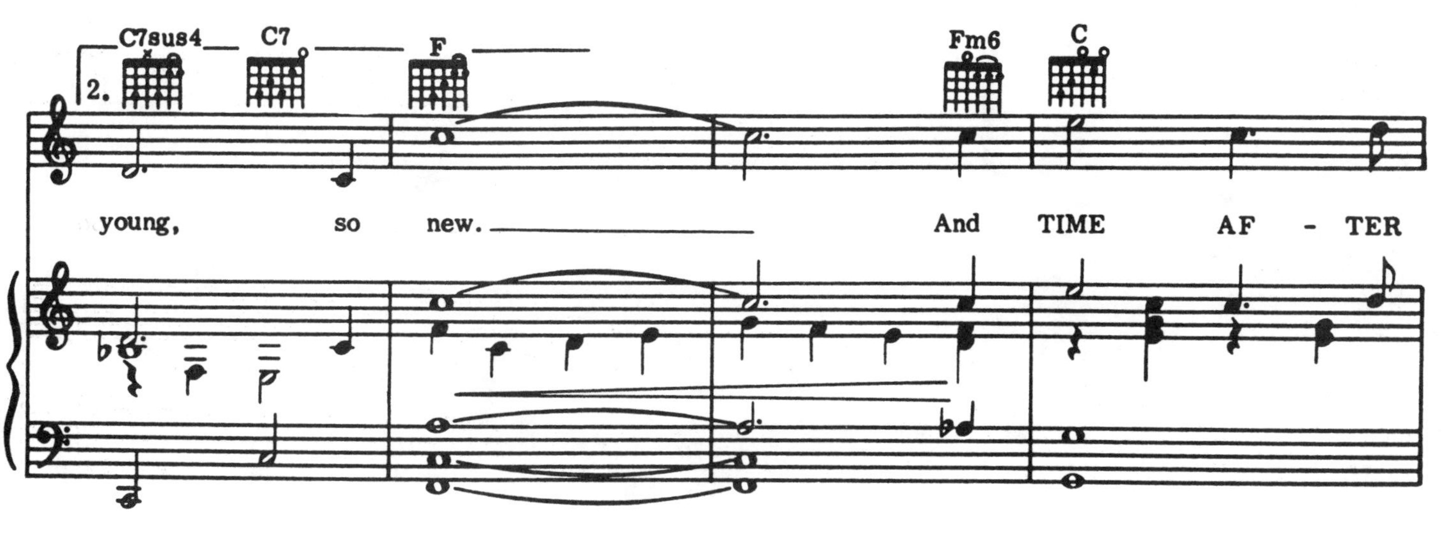
C7sus4
C7
F
Fm6
C
2.
young, so new.
And TIME AF - TER

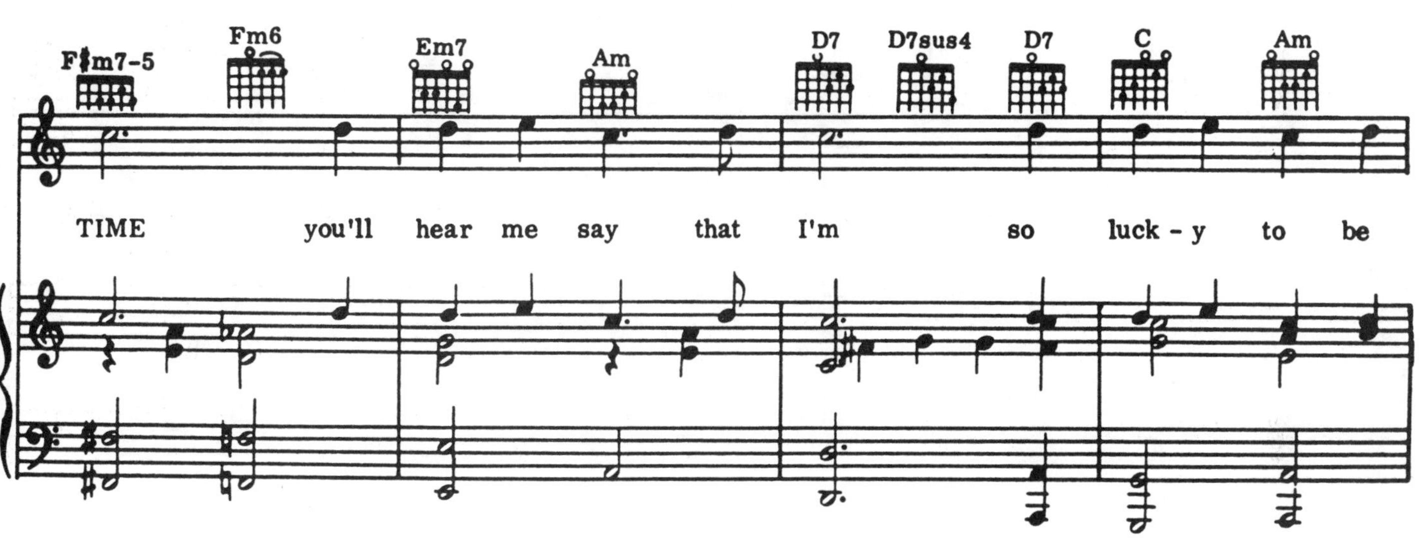
F♯m7-5
Fm6
Em7
Am
D7
D7sus4
D7
C
Am
TIME you'll hear me say that I'm so luck - y to be

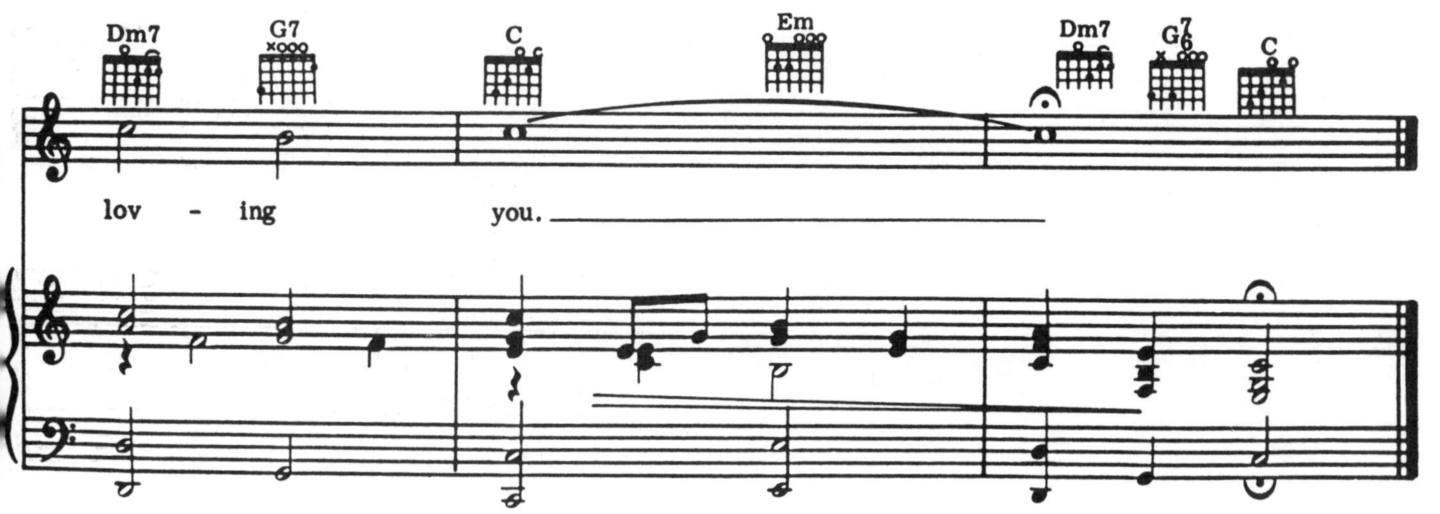
Dm7
G7
C
Em
Dm7
C
lov - ing you.

TILL THEN

In 1944, Sol Marcus' song was recorded by the Mills Brothers on the Decca label, earning a place on ASCAP's Hits Song List that year. It was revived ten years later, in 1954, by Hilltoppers with their best selling Dot recording.

Words and Music by
GUY WOOD, EDDIE SEILER
and SOL MARCUS

Slowly ***(with expression)***

Verse

Gm7 C7 Fmaj.7 F6 F♯dim Gm7 C7 C7+5 F Dm7

My love will leave you "nev - er," so kiss me good-bye and smile; "Till

mp *a tempo*

F7 E7 Am Fm6 C G7 Gm7 C7

then" can't mean for - ev - er, but it cer - tain - ly could mean "a - while."

mf *f*

Refrain

Fmaj.7 F6 Gm7 C9 C7+5 Fmaj.7 F6

TILL THEN my darl - ing please wait for me, TILL THEN no mat - ter

mp

Gm6
A7+5
Edim
B♭6
Bdim
F6
D7♭9
Gm
B♭m
when it will be, one day we'll be to-geth-er a-gain, please wait TILL
C9
Edim
Fmaj.7
F6
Gm7
C9
C7+5
Fmaj.7
F6
THEN. Our dreams will live tho' we are a-part, our love I know will
Gm6
A7+5
Edim
B♭6
Bdim
F6
D7♭9
keep in our hearts, TILL THEN please think of me lov-ing-ly, and
Gm
C9
F
E7
Am
E7
wait for me. Al-though there are o-ceans we must cross, and

Am
Bm7
E7
Am
E7
mountains that we must climb, I know ev-'ry gain must have a loss, so
Am7
Gm7
C9
Edim
Fmaj.7
F6
Gm7
C9
C7+5
pray that our loss is noth-ing but time. TILL THEN let's dream of what there will be, TILL
Fmaj.7
F6
Gm6
A7+5
Edim
B♭6
Bdim
Fmaj.7
Cm6
Adim
THEN we'll call on each mem-o-ry, TILL THEN when I will hold you a-gain, please
mf
1. Gm7
C9
F
D♭7
C7
2. Gm7
C7
F
wait TILL THEN. TILL wait TILL THEN.
rall.
f
8

Ruby Keeler and Lee Dixon

TOO MARVELOUS FOR WORDS

The 1937 Warner Bros. film, Ready, Willing And Able *was the first collaboration between Mercer and Whiting. In the film, Ruby Keeler and Lee Dixon, with dozens of chorines, tap out the lyrics of this tune on a giant typewriter. Bing Crosby's recording that same year reached the top of the charts. Having earned the status of pop standard, this great song could also be heard in the 1950 film* Young Man With A Horn.

Words by
JOHNNY MERCER
Music by
RICHARD A. WHITING

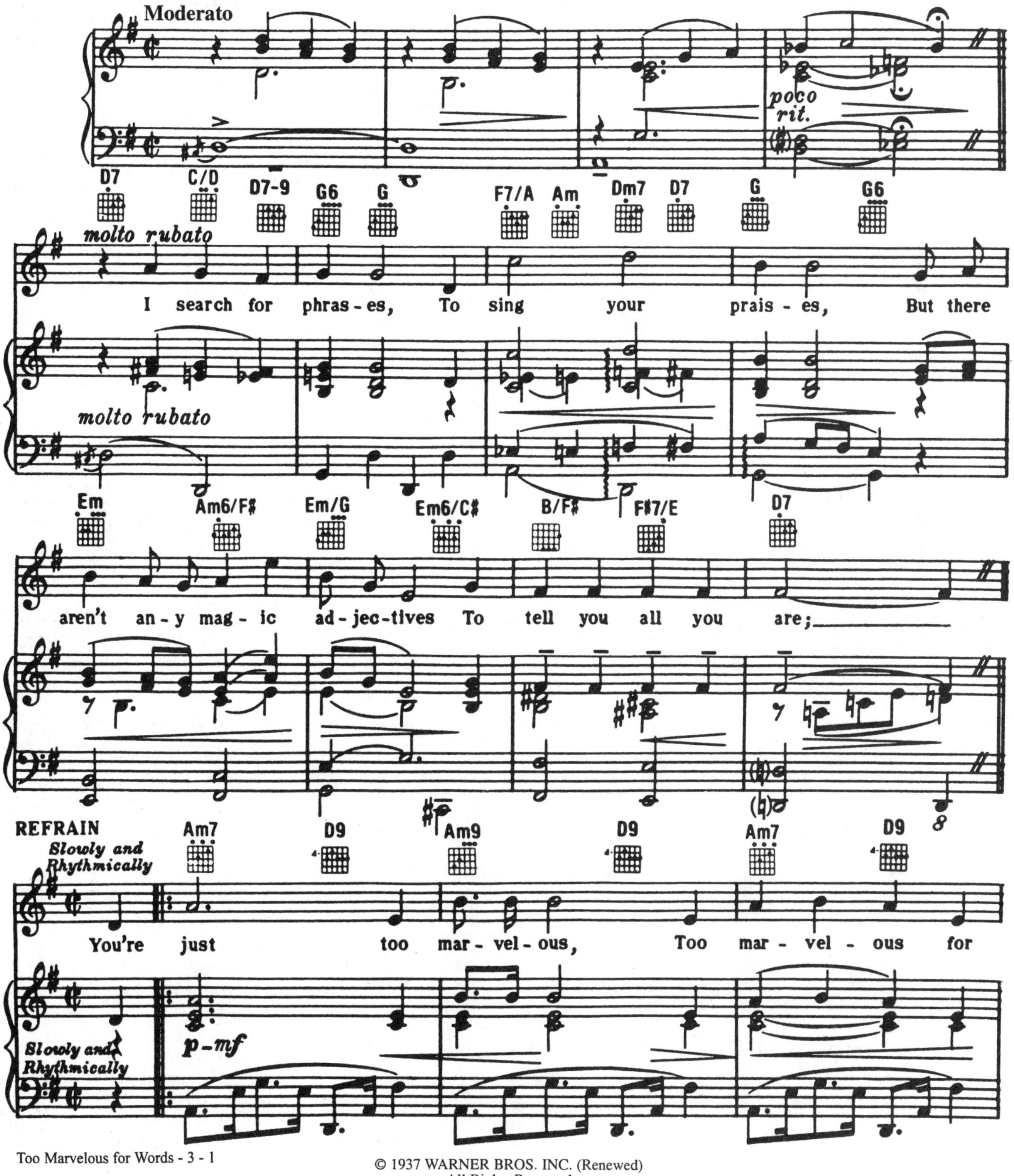

Moderato

poco rit.

D7 C/D D7-9 G6 G F7/A Am Dm7 D7 G G6

molto rubato

I search for phras - es, To sing your prais - es, But there

Em Am6/F# Em/G Em6/C# B/F# F#7/E D7

aren't an - y mag - ic ad - jec - tives To tell you all you are;

REFRAIN

Slowly and Rhythmically

Am7 D9 Am9 D9 Am7 D9

You're just too mar - vel - ous, Too mar - vel - ous for

p-mf

Am9
D9
F#/G
G
G6
C9
G
words, Like glo - ri - ous, glam - our - ous and that old stand - by,
F#/G
G6
Am7
D9
Am9
D9
am - or - ous, It's all too won - der - ful, I'll
Am7
D9
Am9
D9
F#/G
G
G6
F#/G
G
G6
Em6/
nev - er find the words, That say e - nough, tell e - nough, I
B
C#m7
F#9
B
Dm7/G
G9sus
G9
mean, they just aren't swell e - nough, You're much too much, And

Dm6/B
Dm7/A
Fm6/Ab
G+
Cmaj7
G+
C6
G+
just too ver - y ver - y! To ev - - er be in
Cmaj7
C6
G/B
Bbdim7
Am7
D7
Am7
D9
Am9
D9
Web - ster's Dic - tion - a - ry, And so I'm bor - row - ing a
F#/G
G
Dm6/F
Dm/E
E7
E7-9
Em7/A
Edim7/A
Am
Cm6/A
G+/B
love song from the birds, To tell you that you're mar - vel - ous, Too
Cm6
Cm
C
D7
G
G
G6
poco rit.
mar - vel - ous for words. You're words.
dim.
p poco rit.
pp

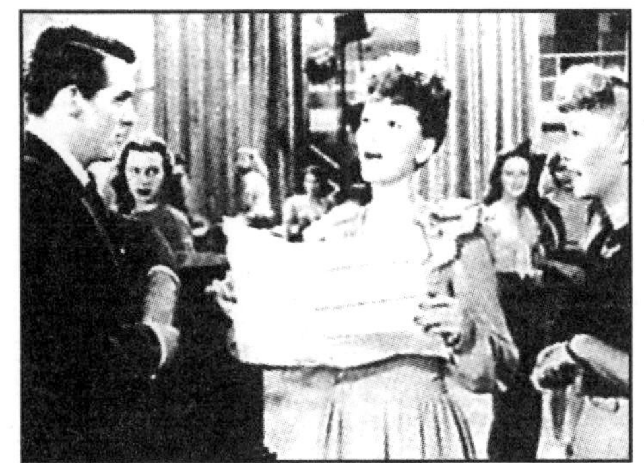

Carry Grant, Mary Martin and Jane Wyman in *Night And Day*

YOU DO SOMETHING TO ME

Although it opened to critical disadmiration, the 1929 Broadway show Fifty Million Frenchmen *soon became a rip-roaring success by the power of word of mouth alone! "You Do Something To Me," a standard from that hit show, was also featured in such films as 1946's* Night And Day, *and 1960's* Can Can.

Words and Music by
COLE PORTER

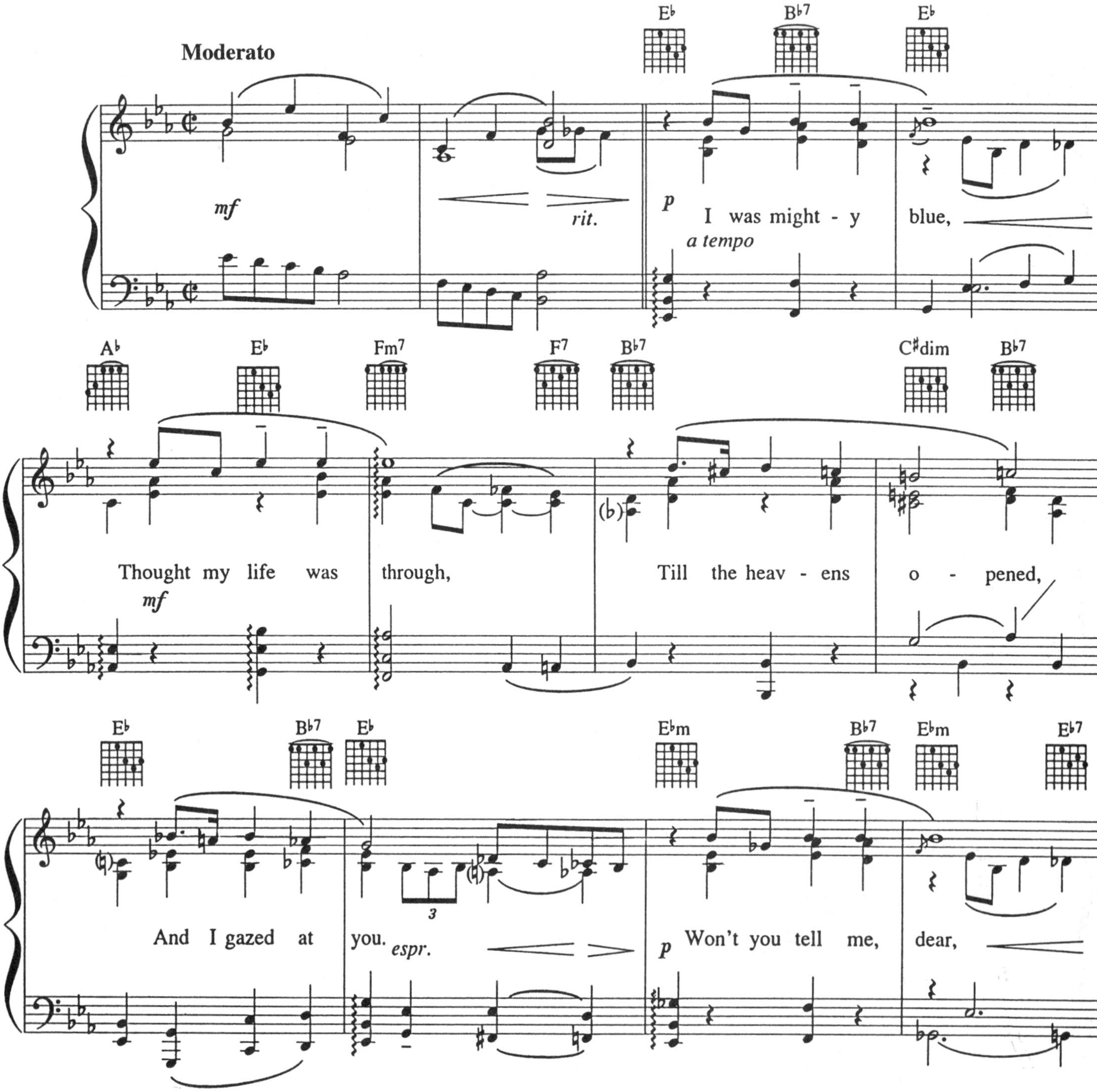

Moderato
E♭ B♭7 E♭
mf
rit.
p
a tempo
I was might - y blue,
A♭ E♭ Fm7 F7 B♭7 C♯dim B♭7
Thought my life was through,
mf
Till the heav - ens o - pened,
E♭ B♭7 E♭ E♭m B♭7 E♭m E♭7
And I gazed at you.
espr.
p
Won't you tell me, dear,

You Do Something to Me - 4 - 1

A♭m
E♭m
F7
Gm
Gm7
Why, when you ap - pear,
mf
Some - thing hap - pens
p
Em7-5
F♯dim
Dm7-5
C7
Fm
B7
B♭7
to me
And the strang - est
feel - ing goes through me?
poco rit.
Slowly, with expression
Refrain
E♭
D
You do some - thing to me.
p - mf
a tempo
B+
Edim
Some - thing that sim - ply mys - ti - fies me.

Fm
Edim
Fm
Tell me, why should it
C7
F7
be You have the pow'r to hyp - no -
B♭7
F♯dim
E♭
tize me? Let
F♯dim
B♭7
C7
me live 'neath your spell,

B
B♭
Edim
A♭
Gm
B♭7
Do do that voo - doo that you do so well, For
mf
E♭
D
E♭
you
p
do
some - thing to
C7
F7
B♭7
me That no - bod - y else could
R.H.
L.H.
mf
1.
E♭
Fm7
B♭7
2.
E♭
do.
do.
p

Vivian Blaine, June Haver and Vera-Ellen

YOU MAKE ME FEEL SO YOUNG

Russian-born Josef Myrow collaborated primarily with Mack Gordon for Fox Studios in Hollywood. Introduced by Vera-Ellen and Charles Smith in Fox's Three Little Girls In Blue, *"You Make Me Feel So Young" is a tribute to the youthful feelings that love inspires. Always the source of such inspiration, Frank Sinatra sent thousands of hearts aflutter with his Capitol recording. (*Songs For Swingin' Lovers, *Capitol SN653)*

Words by
MACK GORDON
Music by
JOSEF MYROW

Medium tempo ***(with a lilt)***

mf

Bb Fdim Cm7 F7 F9+5

You Make Me Feel So Young,

p - mf

Bb Fdim7 3 fr. Fm7 F7 Bb Bb7 3 fr. Bb7+

You make me feel so spring has sprung, And ev - 'ry time I

Ebmaj7 Cm7 Dm7 Gm7 C7 F7

see you grin, I'm such a hap - py in - di-vid - u - al.

Bb Fdim Cm7 F7 Bb Fdim 3 fr.
The mo - ment that you speak, I wan - na go play
Fm7 F7 Bb Bb7 3 fr. Bb7+ Ebmaj7 Cm7
hide and seek, I wan - na go and bounce the moon, just like
Dm7 Gm7 C7 F7 Bb7 Bbdim Bb7 3 fr. Ebdim
a toy bal - loon. You and I are
Bb7 3 fr. Bbdim Fm7 Bb7 3 fr. Ebdim
just like a cou - ple of tots, run - ning a - cross a

Gm7
Bbdim Eb
Cm
G7 Cm
C7
F7 Cm7 F7
Cb
meadow, pick - ing up lots of for - get - me - nots.
Fdim
Cm7
F7
Bb
Fdim7
You Make Me Feel So Young.
You make me feel there are
Fm7
F7
Bb
Bb+7
Ebmaj7
Ebm6
songs to be sung, bells to be rung, and a won - der - ful fling to be
Bb
Dm6 Fdim
Cm7
F7
Bb
Dm6 Fdim
flung.
And e - ven when I'm old and gray,

Cm7
F7
D7+
D7
G7-9
3 fr.
I'm gon-na feel the way I do to - day, 'cause
Cm
G7
Cm
C7
F7
1. B♭
Gm7
Cm7
F7
F7+
You Make Me Feel So Young.
ff
2. B♭
Gm7
Cm7
F7
F7+
B♭
Gm7
Young.
Cm7
F7
F7+
B♭

Judy Garland and Clark Gable

YOU MADE ME LOVE YOU

The most remembered performance of this torch song was by a teen-age Judy Garland singing her heart out to a photograph of every girl's dreamboat, Clark Gable. This segment was included in the film Broadway Melody of 1938 *as an afterthought. Her performance eventually overshadowed every other rendition of this song, with the possible exception of Harry James' recording in 1941.*

Words by
JOE McCARTHY
Music by
JAMES V. MONACO

Bounce tempo

8

Verse

C Cmaj7 Cdim Dm7 G7 C Cmaj7 Cdim

I've been wor - ried all day long, — Don't know if — I'm
I had pic - tured in my mind, — Some day I — would

Dm7 G7 E7 F7 E7 E7 Am Cm6

right or wrong, — I can't help — just what I say, —
sure - ly find, — Some-one hand - some, some-one true, —

G E7 A7 D7 G7 F#7 G7 C Cmaj7 Cdim
Your love makes_ me speak this way._ Why, oh! why_ should
But I nev - er thought of you._ Now my dream_ of
D7 G7 E7 F7 E7
I feel blue?_ Once I used_ to
love is o'er,_ I want you_ and
E7 Am Cm D7 F7 Am F7 D7 F7 Am Cm
laugh at you,_ But now I'm cry-in',_ No use de - ny - in',_ There's no one
noth-ing more,_ Come on en - fold me,_ Come on and hold me,_ Just like you
Bm Cdim A7 D7 G Dm7 G7
else but you_ will do._
nev - er did_ be - fore._

Chorus
C
Cmaj7
C6
C
Cdim
Dm7
Fm6
G7
(slow rhythmic swing)
You Made Me Love You, I did-n't wan-na do it, I
did-n't wan-na do it,
G7
Dm7
G7
B
You made me want you,
C
And all the time you knew it,
I guess you al-ways knew it,
A7
Ab
A7
D7
Am7
Fm7
You made me hap-py some times,
You made me glad,

D7
But there were times dear, You made
R.H.
Dm7 G7 Gb7 G7 C Cmaj7 C6
me feel so bad. You made me
f
p-f
(8) (8)
C Cdim Dm7 Fm6 G7 Dm7 Fm6 G7
sigh for, I did-n't wan-na tell you, I did-n't wan-na tell you,
(8) (8) (8) (8)
G7 Dm7 B7 E7
I want some love that's true, Yes I do, 'Deed I
L.H.
(8) (8)

A7 Edim A7 Edim A7 Ab7 A7
do, You know I do. Gim - me, gim - me what I cry for, You
D7 D7 Fdim D7 D7-5
know you got the brand of kiss - es that I'd die for,
C Fdim Am D7 G7
You know You Made Me Love You.
1. C Am C
You.
F#dim Ab7 G7
2. C
You.
R.H.

Eve Arden, Doris Day and Jack Carson in *My Dream Is Yours*

YOU MUST HAVE BEEN A BEAUTIFUL BABY

Dick Powell sang this song of admiration to Olivia DeHavilland in the 1938 film, Hard To Get. *It wasn't long before Bing Crosby's recording (with brother Bob's orchestra) was the no. 1 hit on the charts, closely followed by the Tommy Dorsey recording. In 1946 it could be heard in* The Eddie Cantor Story, *and in 1946 Doris Day sang it in* My Dream Is Yours. *Vocalist Bobby Darin's hit recording in 1969 reaffirmed the "perennial favorite" status of this tune.*

Words by
JOHNNY MERCER

Music by
HARRY WARREN

Moderato

mp

Eb Ebmaj7 Eb7 C7

Does your moth - er re - al - ize, the stork de - liv - ered quite a prize, the

p molto rubato

F7 Bb9 Bb7 Eb B9 Bb7 Eb Ebmaj7

day he left you on the fam - 'ly tree. Does your dad ap - pre - ci - ate, that

Eb7 D7 Gm 3fr. Gb7 Bb/F F7

you are mere - ly su - per great, the mir - a - cle of an - y cen - tu -

You Must Have Been a Beautiful Baby - 3 - 1

Bb F13 Bb Fm7 F7+5 Bb9
ry, if they don't just send them both to me.
rall.
G7 C Dm7/C D#dim7/C C C+ C7+5 C7-5 F9 Cm7
You Must Have Been A Beau-ti-ful Ba - by, you must have been a won - der - ful child.
p - mf with a lilt
F9 Cm7/G G#m(#7) F9/A Bb9sus Bb9 Fm9 Bb9
When you were on - ly start - in' to go to kin - der - gar - ten, I
Ebmaj7 Ebmaj7/G F#dim7 Fm7 Bb7 G7 C Dm7/C D#dim7/C C
bet you drove the lit - tle boys wild. And when it came to win - ning blue rib -

C+
C7+5
C7-5
F9
Cm7
F9 Cm7/G G#m(#7) F7/A
bons, you must have shown the oth - er kids how, I can
Eb/Bb
Eb+
Eb6
Eb+
Eb
Cm7
see the judg - es eyes as they hand - ed you the prize, I bet you made the cut - est bow.
F13
F#dim7
Eb/G
G7
C7
C7+5 C7
Oh! You Must Have Been A Beau-ti-ful Ba - by, 'cause
F9
Bb9
Bb13
1. Eb
G7
2. Eb
ba - by look at you now. You

Frank Sinatra and Doris Day

YOUNG AT HEART

As a 1939 solo effort by composer Johnny Richards, this tune was orginally titled "Moonbeam" . . . Then along comes Carolyn Leigh in 1953 with a fresh set of lyrics and voilà! A no. 1 gold record for Frank Sinatra is born. The song was featured in Liam O'Brien's great film Young At Heart, *starring Frank Sinatra and Doris Day.*

Words by
CAROLYN LEIGH
Music by
JOHNNY RICHARDS

Slowly

Bb — Edim — Cm7 — F7 — Cm7 — F7 — F9 — F9+5 — Bb

Fair-y tales can come true, it can hap-pen to you if you're Young At Heart. For it's hard, you will find, to be nar-row of mind if you're Young At Heart. You can

Fm6
G7
Fm6
G7
G+
C9
C7
go to ex-tremes with im-pos-si-ble schemes, you can laugh when your dreams fall a-
C9
C7
F7
Bdim
F7
Bdim
F7
Cm7
F9
part at the seams and life gets more ex-cit-ing with each pass-ing day, and
Bb6
F#dim
Bb6
F#7
Cm7
F7
Bb
love is eith-er in your heart or on the way. Don't you know that it's worth ev-'ry
Edim
Cm7
F7
Cm7
trea-sure on earth to be Young At Heart. For, as rich as you are, it's much
p
mp

F7 F9 F9+5 Bb
bet-ter by far to be Young At Heart. And if
p
mp
Fm6 G7 Fm6 G7 G7+5 G7 C9 C7
you should sur-vive to a hun-dred and five look at all you'll de-rive out of
Eb Ebm Bb F7 Cm7 F7
be-ing a-live, and here is the best part, you have a head start
Bb Bb6 Eb6 Edim Cm7 F9 Bb Cm7 F9 Bb
if you are a-mong the ver-y Young At Heart. Fair-y Young At Heart.
mp
f

Ruby Keeler and Warner Baxter in *Forty-Second Street*

YOU'RE GETTING TO BE A HABIT WITH ME

Introduced in the classic 1933 film musical Forty-Second Street *(which became a megahit Broadway production in the '80s), "You're Getting To Be A Habit With Me" was later featured in the 1951 movie musical* Lullaby Of Broadway, *starring Doris Day. Recordings by Fred Waring, Frank Sinatra, Petula Clark, Mel Tormé and Jackie Gleason and his Orchestra all enjoyed success, but it was Bing Crosby who brought it to no. 1 in 1933.*

Lyric by
AL DUBIN
Music by
HARRY WARREN

Moderately

L.H.

mf

rit.

F E F E G7 B♭m C7

I don't know ex - act - ly how it start - ed, but it start - ed in

mp
a tempo

F Gm7 3 fr. C7 F E F E C F♯°7

fun; I just want - ed some - one to be gay with, to

Dm7 G7 Gm7 B♭m C7 F♯°7 Gm Dm
3fr 3fr
play with some - one. But now I re - al - ize that I could
mf colla voce
C♯°7 Dm Fm6 Em A♯°7 Dm Em Gm7 C7 F7
3fr 3fr
nev - er let you go, and I've come to tell you so. Ev - 'ry
poco rit. a tempo
B♭ Dm C7 Am B♭ C7
p - f
kiss, ev - 'ry hug seems to act just like a drug; you're
3 3
F Am F7 B♭ Dm C7 Am
3
get - ting to be a hab - it with me. Let me stay in your arms, I'm ad -